CW00376681

The Unspeakable Girl

THE ITALIAN LIST

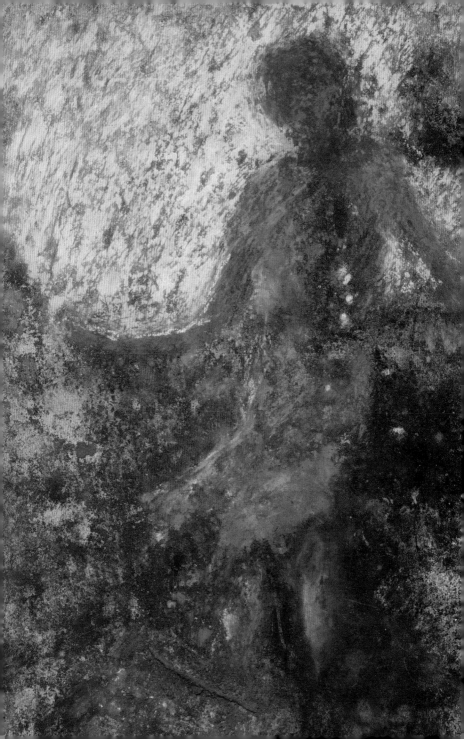

Contents

The Italian List
SERIES EDITOR: ALBERTO TOSCANO

Seagull Books, 2014

La ragazza indicibile. Mito e mistero di Kore
© Giorgio Agamben and Monica Ferrando, 2010

Originally published by Electa, Milan, 2010

English translations © Individual translators, 2014
Images © Monica Ferrando, 2014

ISBN 978 0 8574 2 083 1

First printing 2014
Second printing 2014

British Library Cataloguing-in-Publication Data
A catalogue record for this book is available
from the British Library

Designed by Sunandini Banerjee, Seagull Books, Calcutta, India
Printed and bound by Hyam Enterprises, Calcutta, India

The Unspeakable Girl

The Myth and Mystery of Kore

GIORGIO AGAMBEN
MONICA FERRANDO

TRANSLATED BY LELAND DE LA DURANTAYE
AND ANNIE JULIA WYMAN

LONDON NEW YORK CALCUTTA

THE UNSPEAKABLE GIRL:
THE MYTH AND MYSTERY OF KORE

Giorgio Agamben

I

The fifth-century Alexandrian lexicographer Hesychius refers to a lost play by Euripides in which figures
an 'unspeakable girl' (*arretos kore*). Hesychius explains
that she is none other than Persephone. One of Persephone's more common epithets is 'little girl'. In Plato's
Phaedrus, *korai* is the name given to the small dolls hung
from branches near temples (*Phaedr*us 230). The little
girl, as such, is unspeakable.[1]

In 1941, Karoly Kerényi and Carl Gustav Jung
published in Amsterdam a book entitled *Einführung in
das Wesen der Mythologie* (Introduction to the Essence of
Mythology). A single look at its table of contents suf-
fices to show that the material treated therein hardly
corresponds to the title.[2] The book consists of two

essays. The first is by Kerényi and treats the mythological figure of the divine child (*Das göttliche Kind*) and, through the figure of Kore, the mythological figure of the divine girl (*Das göttliche Mädchen*). This essay is accompanied by two extensive commentaries by Jung on the corresponding psychological archetypes ('Archetypes of Child Psychology' and 'The Psychological Aspects of Kore'). At the time of both its first and second editions, the Netherlands was under Nazi occupation. Republishing the book in Switzerland 10 years later, and thus with the war long over, the authors noted in a short preface that the book was published in the Netherlands during the Second World War but without a date of publication and without the occupying authority being aware of it. It is thus eminently possible that the serious and seemingly scholarly title was an expedient employed to elude the attention of Nazi censors.

Given that the authors did not find themselves in occupied countries nor were themselves considered politically suspect, the reason for concealment could only have lain in the book's subject—a supposition which a careful reading of the book supports. At the heart of Kerényi's and Jung's studies is the figure of the *Urkind*—an originary child seen not only in its male and female aspects but, above all, in its androgyny. Kerényi's study of the *Urkind* ends with the figure of the hermaphrodite Dionysus and the statement: 'This has then been our topic: the original and originary Undifferentiated [*das Ur-Unentschiedene*], the original, originary child [*das Urkind*].'[3] Jung's commentary, in turn, occupies itself at length with 'the hermaphroditism of the child'. Evoking the prevalence of the archetype of the *coniunctio* of male and female, Jung writes that 'the symbol, in its significant functionality, points not towards the past, but towards the future, towards a goal not yet reached [. . .] hermaphroditism has progressively become a redemptive force that supervenes conflict' (that the Nazi censors would not have been pleased to see such a 'symbol' offered to the National Socialist man seems perfectly likely).[4]

Kore, the 'divine girl', however, presents an indetermination that is still more unsettling, for it seems at once to call into question and to annul the distinction between the two essential figures of femininity— woman (or mother) and girl (or virgin). Kerényi specifies that 'virgin' is not to be understood in this context in a physical or even anthropomorphic sense. The

3

'primordial element' represented by the young Persephone (Kore), 'seems to correspond more to the hetaera[5] than to the virgin'.[6] Kerényi cites an inscription
from Delphi in which the two Eleusinian divinities,
Demeter (the woman) and Kore (the daughter), were
paradoxically united—*kai kores / kai gynaikos*, at once
girl and woman. Curiously, however, he interprets this
equation as meaning 'an individual dies and yet lives
on in his or her descendants.'[7] The indetermination
between woman and girl is reduced by Kerényi to a
banality: 'to experience return, apocatastasis of ancestral life, as Professor Jung has framed it, in such a manner that the life of the individual is prolonged in future
generations'.[8]

It was not, however, ideas such as the return of
ancestral life or the survival of the individual through
his or her descendants that would have disturbed Nazi
censors (or, for that matter, today's moralists and legis-
lators, who are in the process of unwittingly transform-
ing the figure of the child into a prohibited—and
thus privileged—sexual object). What would have been
disturbing for the censors would have been the
indetermination of the *Urkind* with respect to man
and Kore–Demeter with respect to woman. Of the

Eleusinian Demeter, the scandalized Church Father Clement of Alexandria asked, 'Am I to call her mother or wife (*metros e gynaikos*)?'[9] *Kai kores / kai gynaikos*— between daughter and mother, virgin and woman, the 'unspeakable girl' presents a third figure which puts into question all we think we know about femininity, and all we think we know about man and woman.

The Greek term *kore* (masculine form: *koros*) does not refer to a precise chronological age. Derived from a root meaning 'vital force', it refers to the principle that makes both plants and animals grow (*koros* also means 'offshoot' in the botanical sense). A *kore* can thus be old, like the Phorcydes, called *denaiai korai*, the 'long-lived girls' and the *graiai*, 'those with white hair'.[10] Aeschylus calls the terrifying avengers of blood crime, the Erinyes (or Furies), *korai*, as well as *graiai palaiai paides* (ancient children with white hair) (*Eumenides* 68–69). It is telling in this regard that the rage and the implacable pursuit of vengeance which the tragic hero—and, in *The Eumenides*, Athena and Apollo—seek by every means to domesticate are embodied by children. One of these 'aged girls'—benevolent this time—is Iambe, who appears in the myth of Persephone, of Kore—the *girl* par excellence. Kore is life in

6

so much as it does not allow itself to be 'spoken', in so much as it cannot be defined by age, family, sexual identity or social role.

II

Erwin Rohde claimed that the Eleusinian mystery cult consisted of dramatic action or, more precisely, of a sort of 'pantomime accompanied by sacred chants and formulae' representing 'the sacred story of the rape of Kore, the wanderings of Demeter and the reunion of the two goddesses'.[11] Clement of Alexandria defined the Eleusinian mystery cult as *drama mystikon* or 'initiatory drama'.[12]

The verb *myein*, 'to initiate', means etymologically, 'to close'—notably the eyes but, more importantly, the mouth. At the beginning of the sacred rites, the herald would 'command silence' (*epitattei ten siopen*).

In his version of 'Eleusinia', Giorgio Colli asked what meaning the requirement of secrecy for initiates into the Eleusinian mysteries could have had so that the entire Athenian population was eligible for initiation.[13]

The source materials make clear that everyone, including slaves, was eligible for initiation (as long as they had not defiled themselves through a blood crime). Colli, for his part, stresses that the officiating families of the Eumolpidae and the Kerykes undertook a careful selection of initiates, at least for the 'grand mysteries', culminating in what was called the *epopteia* or 'vision'.

It is nevertheless possible that the point of the silence was not to keep the uninitiated ignorant but intended for the benefit of the initiates themselves. In other words, it is possible that those who had been given an experience of the unknowable—or, at least, the *discursively* unknowable—were encouraged to refrain from attempting to put into words what they had seen and felt.

Clement of Alexandria was either himself initiated into the mystery cult at Eleusis or was told of the process by more or less reliable sources. He relates that, at Eleusis, the hierophant presented the initiate with a cut ear of wheat and recited the formula *hye, kye* ('rain', 'render fertile'). 'And this was the grand and inexpressible Eleusinian mystery,' he contemptuously writes.[14] In so doing, Clement displays the degree to which he had lost all sense of the role and meaning of the unspeakable in pagan religion. Through the mystery cults one was not held to learn something—such as a secret doctrine—about which one had to then remain silent. Instead, the initiate was meant to ecstatically experience his or her own silencing—*mega gar ti theon sebas ischanei auden* ('when confronted with the gods great wonder silences the voice'; *Homeri Hymnus in Cererem* 5.479). The initiate was thus to experience the power and potentiality offered to mankind of the 'unspeakable girl'—the power and potentiality of a joyfully and intransigently *in-fantile* existence.[15]

As Rohde remarked: '[I]t was impossible to reveal "the mystery" because there was nothing to reveal.'[16]

In light of the preceding it should come as no surprise that, in Greek, the expression for 'divulging the mystery' is *exorchesthai ta mysteriai*—literally, 'dance it away' or 'dance it out', which also means 'fake it' or 'imitate it poorly'. What is more, in the *Hymn to Demeter*, it is said of the *orgia kala* ('sacred ritual') that it is not possible to 'seek to know' (*pynthestha* or 'proffer (*acheein*) them' (*Homeri Hymnus in Cererem* 5.479).

At two points in esoteric dialogues which have been lost, Aristotle compared philosophical wisdom (*theoria*) to mystical vision. The first of these was in

Eudemus where we read that 'those who have directly touched (*thigountes aplos*) pure truth claim to possess philosophy's ultimate term (*telos echein philosophias*), as in an initiation (*hoion en teletei*)' (*Eudemus* frag. 10). It was, however, in *De philosophia*, that Aristotle makes the comparison most comprehensively. Therein, Aristotle affirms that 'the initiates do not have to learn something (*mathein ti*), but that, after having become capable (*genomenous epitedeious*), they experience and are disposed to it (*pathein kai diatethenai*)' (*De philosophia* frag. 15). In that same work, Aristotle distinguishes between 'that which is proper to teaching (*to didaktikon*) and that which is proper to initiation (*to telestikon*). The first comes through listening; the second comes only when the intellect itself is illuminated (*autou pathontos nou ten ellampsin*).' Michael Psellos, the source for this fragment, tells us that this second element 'was also called by Aristotle the mystical (*mysteriodes*) element, similar to the Eleusinian initiations, in that the initiate receives not instruction (*ou didaskamenos*) but an impression (*typoumenos*).'[17]

It is important to eschew the facile interpretation of these passages which would have Aristotle veiling *theoria* in clouds of mysticism and, instead, to carefully analyse them. This is necessary not only to understand Aristotle's sense of supreme philosophical wisdom but also for the light they cast on the essence of mystical initiation. We should begin by noting that the terminology of fragment 15 is genuinely Aristotelian. Contrary to the claims of Ulrich von Wilamowitz-Moellendorff, who would exclude *diatethenai* as non-Aristotelian, the pairing of the concepts *pathein* and *diatethenai* is authentically Aristotelian and is employed in a similar manner by Aristotle in *De anima* (414a11). What is more, the connection between the two is seen in Aristotle's *Metaphysica Delta* where *diathesis*, *hexis* and *pathos* are clearly linked. Disposition (*diathesis*) is defined here as a type of habitus (*hexis*): 'That in virtue of which something is disposed to be good or bad, be it in relation to itself or in relation to something else' (1022b1–20).

If we recall the decisive role that the concepts of *pathos* and *hexis* play in Aristotle's theory of knowledge as it is put forth in *De anima*, this fragment proves singularly illuminating (417a10–417b15). Aristotle distinguishes between two meanings for the term *paschein*. The first refers to someone in the process of learning something (*dia matheseos*), for whom 'to undergo' implies the sense of 'destruction through the working of an opposing principle or concept'. The second refers to someone who has already become familiar with a certain subject matter and for whom 'to undergo' implies 'the conservation (*soteria*) of potentiality in an act that is similar to it'. In the second case, 'he who has a certain knowledge becomes a knower in act (*theoroun*), and this is not an alteration because there is increase (*epidosis* or supplementary gift) both towards oneself and towards the act' (417b2–7).

The two modes of *theoria* described here correspond exactly to the two types of knowledge presented in fragment 15: the didactic (*didaktikon*), and the initiatory (*telestikon*). Aristotle affirms this without reservation in a passage which may be considered an allusion to *De philosophia*: 'The intelligent and thinking being should call that which leads from potentiality to actuality not learning (*didaskalia*) but by another name (*eteran eponymian*)' (417b9–11). In the esoteric dialogue, this 'other name' is drawn precisely from the language of the mystery cults—*to telestikon*, 'the initiatory'.

According, thus, to the testimony of Aristotle, that which the initiate experienced at Eleusis was not irrational ecstasy but a vision analogous to *theoria*, to supreme philosophical knowledge. What in both cases is essential was that the experience in question no longer concerned material which was learnt as much as it did a manner of experiencing, a way of undergoing, a giving of self and a completion of thought (Themistius glosses the Aristotelian term *epidosis*—increase—with *teleiosis*—completion—the term with which Christians designed baptismal initiation). And it was this completion of thought that Aristotle, at two decisive instances in *Metaphysics* (1051b24, for the knowledge of simple things, and 1072b21, for the intellect that thinks of itself) expresses through the term *thigein* (touch) which, in the fragment cited from *Eudemus*, is compared to the experience of initiates.

It is the first of these two passages that allows us to better understand the unspeakable present in the mystery cults. This unspeakablility was not a prohibition concerning the communication of a secret doctrine, nor did it concern some impossibility of speaking. Christian chroniclers note the ritual formulae pronounced by the initiates, such as 'I have fasted', 'I have drunk the *kykeon*'[18] or 'I have taken the *kiste* (box), taken from the *kiste*, and after working on it have put it back in the *kalathos* (open basket).' And we have already seen the formula of the hierophant, *hye, kye* ('rain', 'render fertile') to which may be added one reported by Hippolytus: 'The Mistress has given birth to a Holy Boy! Brimo has given birth to Brimos! That is, the Strong One to the Strong One.'[19] Even if these relatively late reports from biased parties may be inexact, scholars are in agreement that the ceremony did not take place in absolute silence.

In *Metaphysics*, Aristotle says that, in knowing uniform things, the truth lies in *theigein kai phanai*, in 'touching and naming', and immediately specifies that 'naming' (*phasis*, the offering of words not linked in the form of a judgement) is not the same as 'proposition' (*kataphasis*, saying something about something) (1051b22–4). The knowledge conveyed at Eleusis could thus be expressed in names but not in propositions; the 'unspeakable girl' could be *named* but not *said*. In the mystery cult, there is thus no place for the *logos apophantikos* (assertion) (*De interpretatione* 17b8) but only for the *onoma* (the name). And in the name is something like a 'touching' and a 'seeing'.

By likening philosophical knowledge to the mystery cults, Aristotle was returning to and taking up a Platonic motif. In *Symposium*, Diotima speaks of love's 'mysteries' (*telea*) and 'initiatory visions' (*epoptika*); she affirms that in love's mysteries there will not be 'either discourse or science' (*oude tis logos oude tis episteme*) and that beauty 'renders itself visible for itself and with itself in a single eternal vision' (209e, 211b). In *Phaedrus*, the philosopher is compared to 'a man ceaselessly initiated into perfect mysteries' (*telous aei teletas teloumenos*) (this means that, in ancient Greece, philosophy seemed to locate itself with respect to mystical experience, just as, later, it sought its legitimation with respect to religion as *vera religio*) (249c–d).

When she was abducted by Hades, Kore was 'playing (*paizousan*) with the girls of Ocean' (*kouresi syn Okeanou*; *Homeri Hymnus in Cererem* 5.5). That a girl at play became the ideal figure for the supreme initiation and the completion of philosophy, the figure for something that is at once thought and initiation and thus unspeakable—this is the 'mystery'.

III

In the oldest surviving source materials, the result of initiation into the Eleusinian mysteries is expressed in general terms—those of happiness and hope. 'Happy (*olbios*) among humans who live on earth, those who were admitted to the rite!' (*Homeri Hymnus in Cererem* 5.479). 'Blessed is he who has seen these things [the Eleusinian mysteries] before he descends beneath the hollow earth; for he understands the end of mortal life, and the beginning given by Zeus' (Pindar, frag. 137). 'Thrice blessed (*triolbioi*) are those mortals who descend to Hades after having contemplated these mysteries; only they can expect to live there; for those who have not will find only evils' (Sophocles, frag. 387). *Olbios* means happy, blessed and fortunate in all senses, even the most profane (*eis olbeian balle* or 'go happily' meant, ironically, 'go to your ruin'). Aristides and Isocrates speak in this regard of 'sweet hopes' (*edious echein tas elpidas*).

The general idea seems little more than a play on words—the inititates into the mystery cult have a complete life (*telein* means complete, finish and 'initiate'; *tele* means 'mysteries', being merely the plural of *telos*, 'end' or 'goal'). Non-initiates (*ateleis* or the 'incomplete') lead a vain existence, lacking a *telos*. For this reason, in Polygnotus' fresco of Lake Avernus, the non-initiates—depicted as an old man, a boy, a girl and an old woman—carry water in broken pitchers to a jar with a hole in it.

In this regard, Diogenes' irreverence is, as always, instructive. To the Athenians who suggested that he have himself initiated (*myethenai*) because privileged places (*proedriai*, literally, 'first place in line') awaited initiates in Hades, he responded, 'It would be absurd if Agesilaos and Epaminandos are to lie in the mud while utterly worthless people, just because they have been initiated, are to dwell on the Isles of the Blest!' (Diogenes, *Laertius* 6.39).

The Eleusinian myth of Demeter clearly contains comic elements. While the goddess wanders, grief-stricken by the loss of Persephone, she encounters a woman named Baubo, her husband Dysaules and their children Triptolemus, Eumolpos and Eubuleus.

Baubo welcomes the goddess warmly and offers her *kykeon*. Demeter is inconsolable and refuses. Baubo then places herself in front of Demeter and promptly raises her skirts, displaying her genitals and revealing the face of the child Iacchus. The goddess then bursts out laughing and accepts the drink.

Recalling that Iacchus, the divine child of Eleusis, is another name for Dionysus, Kerényi remarks, 'It would be difficult to say what Demeter saw in Baubo's revealed lap. Here we touch upon that which is untellable in the mystery cults.'[20] What is certain is that Demeter sees something that makes her laugh, that the sight was at once obscene and comic. And it is in commemoration of this scene that the initiates say, 'I have fasted, I have drunk the *kykeon*.' Contrary to Clement of Alexandria's malevolent insinuation that the mystery cults 'make tragedies (*ektragodousai*)' out of a rape, it bears recalling that the Eleusinian spectacle—that is, if we can speak of a spectacle—was *comic*, not tragic.[21]

In the *Hymn to Demeter*, in which Baubo does not appear, the role of the buffoonish consoler falls to Iambe, who, through jokes that follow a comic arc, first makes the frowning goddess smile (*meidesai*) and then makes her laugh (*gelasai*), thus restoring Demeter to good humour (*ilaon . . . thymon*; *Homeri Hymnus in Cererem* 55.202–203) (according to some, the expression *polla parascoptosa* or 'making many jokes / jests' was a euphemism for a sort of obscene dance akin to Baubo's gesture).

In any event, Demeter, who has lost hope, experiences a sort of comic initiation when she sees something that restores her to joy and hope. The sequence in the mystery cult's spectacle from which the initiates depart gladdened and with 'sweeter hopes' thus reproduces, in a certain sense, the initiation of Demeter in which Baubo (mother of Eumolpus) and Iambe (of the House of Keleos, and whose descendants were responsible, along with the House of Eumolpus, for the Eleusinian rites) act as hierophants and clowns.

IV

In 1921, in Maria Laach Abbey in the German Rhineland, an obscure Benedictine monk named Odo Casel published *Die Liturgie als Mysterienfeier* (Liturgy as Mystery Celebration), a sort of manifesto for what would become the Liturgical Movement and come to exercise, under this name, an enormous influence within the Catholic Church. According to Casel, the true nature of the Christian liturgy was misunderstood so long as it was not seen that the liturgy was in its essence not doctrine but mystery, and that, as such, it stood in a genetic relationship to the pagan, Eleusinian, Orphic and Hermetic mystery cults. As early as his dissertation of 1918, published as *De philosophorum graecorum silentio mystico*, the young monk showed that the pagan mystery cults did not possess a secret doctrine that could be expressed in words and which it was forbidden to reveal.

Originally, 'mystery' simply meant gestures, acts and words through which divine action was effectively realized in time and in the world for the salvation of mankind. In the same manner, the Christian liturgy is also a 'mystery celebration' in which the redemptive work of Christ is rendered present in and through the Church. According to Casel, the expression 'mystical presence' is a tautology because presence is part of the very essence of the liturgical mystery. What is rendered present in this mystery is not so much Christ as a historical individual as is his 'saving act' (*Heilstat*), communicated through the sacrament. 'The most authentic force of the Catholic liturgy lies in its being the objective mystery and the fullness of actuality (*Wirklichkeiterfülltes*) of the saving action of Christ.'[22]

The 'fullness of actuality' of which Casel speaks is that which the theological tradition attached to the doctrine of the efficacy *ex opere operato* of the liturgical act. This meant, hypothetically speaking, that if the priest who administered the sacrament to a woman did it with the intention of sexually abusing her, or was drunk, or distracted by sinful thoughts, the saving power of the sacrament was unaffected—because that effective power did not depend upon the celebrant but on Christ (which is to say on the 'mystical presence'). The efficacy of the Christian mysteries is guaranteed in any event and every possible situation because it is not the work of man—it is the work of God.

Nothing is farther from this irreducible liturgical operativity than what we find in the pagan mysteries. When Lucius, at the end of *The Golden Ass*, describes his initiation into the mystery cult of Isis, he defines the salvation found there as 'precarious' (*ad instar voluntariae mortis et precariae salutis*).[23] There is no certainty here, only a hesitant movement through the darkness and half-light, on a path suspended between the infernal and supernal gods. These gods appear in dreams and the salvation they offer is precarious because they are offered in an indistinct and perplexing realm, where the distinctions between the high and the low, shadow and light, waking and sleeping, have grown uncertain.

In Latin, *praecarius* means that which is obtained through a *praex*, a verbal request, distinct in this from a *quaestio*, a request which can be made by any and all means and one that would serve to assure its granting (for this reason, the term *quaestio* came to designate 'torture'—that through which one always obtains that which one requests).

If the Christian mystery is, in this sense, always effective, precariousness is the adventurous and nocturnal dimension in which the pagan initiate moves.

Apuleius' novel is the only document from antiquity that offers an extensive description of a mystery cult initiation. That it is from a novel, however, has meant that scholars have not always taken it fully into account. And yet, as can be seen through the remarkable insights of Gianni Carchia, not only is there an essential connection between the novel form and the mystery cults, it is also the novel form which best conveys the meaning of the mystery.[24] For, perhaps, the first time the novel presents the human and earthly element as the vehicle, even if in parodic form, of divine incident in such a manner that the anxieties and qualms, the hopes and the strivings of the initiatory practice correspond exactly to the adventures and misadventures of the protagonist. The interweaving of situation and event, relation and circumstance, that the novel rings round a character is that which makes the character's life like a mystical experience which we are meant not to explain so much as to contemplate, as one would an initiation. If there is somewhere today where an echo of the ancient mysteries can then be heard, it is not in the liturgical splendour of the Catholic Church but in the extreme life resolutions offered by the novel form. Whether it be Lucius in *The Golden Ass* or Isabel Archer in Henry James' *Portrait of a Lady‡*, the novel places us before a *mysterion* in which life itself is at once that which initiates us and that into which we are initiated.

V

What the initiates experience during the Eleusinian rite is always expressed through the verb 'to see' (*opopen*: *Homeri Hymnus in Cererem* 5.480; *idon*: Pindar, frag. 137; *derchthentes*: Sophocles, frag. 837). And 'vision' (*epopteia*) is the term used to designate the supreme stage of initiation. *Epoptes*, 'initiate', also meant 'spectator', and the mysteries that the initiate contemplated were 'living paintings' composed of gestures (*dromena*), words (*legomena*) and the presentation of objects (*deiknymena*).

It is from this angle that we may see the importance of the connection between mystery cults and painting, so alive in Renaissance art and to which Edgar Wind dedicated a now famous book. If the philosophical tradition linked supreme knowledge to mystery visions, if this knowledge had not a discursive character but was experienced through seeing, touching and naming, then painting offered to this knowledge perhaps the most apt expression.

The studies of the Warburg school have confirmed this hypothesis. We must nevertheless beware a danger that even the most astute scholars have not always successfully avoided. According to Wind, 'an iconographer trying to reconstruct the lost argument of a Renaissance painting' is confronted with a paradoxical task: '[T]o remove the veil of obscurity which not only distance in time (although in itself sufficient for that purpose) but a deliberate obliqueness in the use of metaphor has spread over some of the greatest Renaissance paintings'. The scholar must, therefore, learn more than the painter himself could have known about the hidden arguments and meanings. Even though these works were the fruit of a culture that regarded obscurity and mystery as necessary, the iconographer 'must strive for clarity' against the intentions of the artist, because, 'aesthetically speaking, there can be no doubt that the presence of unresolved residues of meaning is an obstacle to the enjoyment of art'.[25]

In contradistinction to this idea, it is important to recall that the allegories of Lorenzo Lotto or Titian, like the Eleusinian mysteries, are not 'mysterious' because they have a concealed doctrinal content that the agility of the interpreter must bring to light but because in them form and content, as at Eleusis, have become indistinguishable. The third element—neutralizing the distinction between form and content—is mysterious because in it there is no longer anything to conceal. Independent of the ideas of patrons and scholars of the period, these images have reached the point at which, because there is nothing left to say on the discursive level, thought and vision coincide. Form and content coincide not because the content now appears unveiled but because, as in the literal meaning of the Latin verb *concidere*, they 'fall together', are reduced and reconciled. What we are then given to contemplate is pure appearance. The little unspeakable girl shows herself.

It is for this reason that we cannot discursively present the knowledge depicted in such paintings; it can, at most, be named in a title.

If it is true that Renaissance allegories offer a richer expression of thought than many contamporaneous philosophical treatises, then not only is painting returned, in such a perspective, to its true theoretical foundations but the very nature of thought is illuminated. Perhaps the canvases of Botticelli and Titian, far from needing to be clarified through the writings of Ficino and Pico, aid us, on the contrary, in understanding the thoughts that those treatises were not able to adequately express. As Kerényi wrote: 'In Botticelli's painting [*The Birth of Venus*] there is as much live mythology as in a Homeric hymn.'[26]

Wind has shown how, through Plotinus and Proclus, the pagan mystical tradition exercised a decisive influence on the leaders of German Idealism, particularly in how Hegel and Schelling conceived of the dialectical movement of thought after the model of *coincidentia oppositorum*. Schelling, who compares this movement to the 'Osirean mysteries' in which what is at issue is the fragmentation and recomposition of a body or a god, cites (in Friedrich Heinrich Jacobi's translation) a passage from Bruno where 'the profoundest mysteries of art' consist in conceiving at once the extreme discrepancy of opposed elements and their point of coincidence. The third element, in which opposites meet, cannot be of the same nature as them and requires a different form of exposition, one in which the opposing elements are at once maintained and neutralized. It is the content but nothing contains it; it is form but it no longer forms anything—exposing, thereby, itself.

The idea of an image philosophy that Walter Benjamin seemed at times to evoke is not a metaphor; on the contrary, it is to be taken literally. The 'image of thought', like Renaissance allegory, is a mystery wherein that which cannot be discursively presented shines for a moment out of the ruins of language.

VI

In a poem entitled 'Eleusis', dedicated to his friend Hölderlin, the 27-year-old Hegel invoked Ceres ('you who reigned in Eleusis') and 'the profundity of the unspeakable sentiment (*unaussprechlichen Gefühles Tiefe*)' out of respect for which the initiate, to whom verbal discourse appears full of failing, 'closes the mouth'. In the lines that follow, 'that which the initiate forbids himself' becomes the task of philosophy. So as not to become 'the plaything and ware of the sophist', the speaker watches over through memory 'that which was seen, heard, felt in the sacred night' and which, isolated from its meaning, survives only 'in the echo of foreign tongues'.[27]

Ten years later, at the beginning of *Phenomenology of Spirit*, Hegel again evokes the Eleusinian mysteries. This time, however, the *pathos* of the unspeakable cedes to a more disenchanted and nearly ironic vision in

which, alongside the initiates, even the animal kingdom
seems to participate in this mystical wisdom:

> In this respect we can tell those who assert the
> truth and certainty of the reality of sense-
> objects that they should go back to the most
> elementary school of wisdom, viz. the ancient
> Eleusinian Mysteries of Ceres and Bacchus,
> and that they have still to learn the secret
> meaning of the eating of bread and the drink-
> ing of wine. For he who is initiated into these
> Mysteries not only comes to doubt the being
> of sensuous things, but to despair of it; in part
> he brings about the nothingness of such things
> himself in his dealings with them, and in part
> he sees them reduce themselves to nothing-
> ness. Even the animals are not shut out from
> this wisdom but, on the contrary, show them-
> selves to be most profoundly initiated into it;
> for they do not just stand idly in front of sen-
> suous things as if these possessed intrinsic
> being, but, despairing of their reality, and
> completely assured of their nothingness, they
> fall to without ceremony and eat them up.
> And all Nature, like the animals, celebrates

these open Mysteries which teach the truth about sensuous things.[28]

Colli has the merit of presenting the fruitful intuition that the cult of Demeter involved a 'close relationship between the divine and the animal spheres'.[29] The figure of Demeter, invoked at Eleusis as *potnia* or 'lady' alluded to the Arcadian cult of the 'lady of the animals'. The origin of the unspeakability in question can thus be sought 'in a certain initial element of the myth' concerning 'the coupling in various forms of god with animal': bull and Pasiphaë on Crete; Poseidon (in the form of a horse) and Demeter in Arcadia; Zeus who, in the form of a serpent, couples with Rhea and, later, with Persephone.[30] What is more, if we accept the identification of Dionysus with the Minotaur, 'we might assert that the daughter of the Arcadian coupling, Despoina-Kore, by uniting with serpent Zeus in the Eleusinian coupling, gave birth to the same son, in the brutally conjoined form of man-animal, already born of the primordial Cretan pairing: Dionysus, the god "of many names"'.[31]

According to ancient testimony and modern scholarship, Dionysus was present at Eleusis. In Sophocles, Iacchus, who appears in the stories of Demeter, is already identified with Dionysus. And, as Colli writes, Dionysus 'is not a man: he is an animal as well as a god, thereby embodying the two terminal points of the human spectrum'.[32]

The Greek word for animal, *zoon*, means, literally, 'living being'. And for a Greek, a god was a 'living being' (even if the god's *zoe* is *ariste kai aidios*, 'optimal and eternal'). In their 'animal' nature—which is to say, their *living* nature—man and god commune. This is the reason gods take on animal form when they desire sexual union with humans.

According to Xenocrates, one of the three laws transmitted by Triptolemus at Eleusis was 'do not harm animals (*zoa me synesthai*).' Rohde is wrong to claim in this connection that 'it is inconceivable that, at Eleusis, the initiates would have imposed, on the Orphic model, perpetual abstinence from all meat [. . .] It is, moreover, possible that the precept (that does not speak precisely of the slaughter of animals) had another meaning and was meant to encourage farmers [. . .] to treat their animals with care.'[33]

This precept has been read in relation to the other of Triptolemus' laws mentioned by Xenocrates, such as that of 'honouring the gods with the fruits of the earth (*theous karpois agallein*)'. In Greece, the economy of the relationship between man and the divine was governed by animal sacrifice. Man is the living being that kills other living beings so as to define his relationship to the divine. During initiation at Eleusis, there were no sacrifices (*agallein* does not belong to the vocabulary of sacrifice and means, 'adorn, give joy') because what was in question was the threshold leading from animal to man (and god), the threshold leading from man (and god) to animal. The 'unspeakable girl' *is* this threshold. Just as she breaks down the barrier between woman and child, virgin and mother, so too does she break down the barrier separating the animal from the divine.

In the Orphic sources, Kore has horns (*keroessa*; *Hymni Orphici* 29.11). And Zeus rapes her in the form of a serpent (*biasamenos kai tauten en drakontos schemati*).

The Greeks experienced the animal and the divine but not the human as a separate and autonomous sphere. Christ separated us from the animal and the divine, thereby condemning us to humanity.

In the mystery cults, the Greeks experienced the extremes of the human condition—the divine and the animal. And, without the mystery cults, these extremes would have been, for them, unthinkable. The living being lost in the animal rediscovered himself in the divine as he who was lost in the divine rediscovered himself in the animal. This is the meaning of the Cretan labyrinth, at the centre of which the hero encounters Asterius the Minotaur—a man with a bull's head.

Rohde warns of 'certain modern mythologists and historians' for whom the Eleusinian mysteries are an enactment of

> a Greek 'natural religion' which they believe they have discovered, in which Demeter would be the earth, Kore-Persephone, her daughter, the seed, the rape and return of Kore, the planting of the seed in the earth and the subsequent emergence of the shoot from the depths—or, in a broader version— 'the annual decline and renewal of vegetation' [. . .] an image of the destiny of the human soul, disappearing only to live anew.[34]

This interpretation is so tenacious that, after being taken up by Frazer in *The Golden Bough*, it appears in even more refined form in *Einführung in das Wesen der Mythologie* (1951), where Kerényi, concerning Kore, speaks of 'the abyss of the seed', symbol of that which transcends the individual, and of the unending cycle of life rising from

death.[35] And yet, this seemingly more profound interpretation also has the defect of presuming a concealed
content of which the myth would be but the cipher.

> Life, because it is an initiation (*myesis*) and the
> most perfect mystical rite (*teleten teleiotaten*),
> should be full of serenity and joy [. . .] In the
> initiations we sit in religious silence (*euphemoi*)
> and in harmonious order. It occurs to no one
> to complain during the initiation or to groan
> when watching the Pythian games or when
> drinking to Cronus. In fact, we contaminate
> these celebrations that the god stages and
> in which we are initiated by living amongst
> bitter lament, preoccupation and breathless
> anxiety (*Peri philosophias* frag. 14).

We are to live life like an initiation. But to what?
Not to a doctrine but to life itself and its absolute
absence of mystery. There is no mystery. There is an
unspeakable girl.

We differ from other animals in that we are initiated into our lives. Which is to say, we must first lose
ourselves in the human so as to rediscover ourselves as
alive, and vice-versa.

Translated by Leland de la Durantaye

47

Notes

1   It should be noted that neither the Greek term nor
    the Italian one with which the author translates it
    possesses the English word's suggestion of impish
    or malicious misbehaviour. Given the alternative
    between the idiomatic *unspeakable* and the calque
    unsayable, I deemed the former truer to the original.
    —Trans.

2   An English translation of the book was published in
    1951 under the title *Essays on a Science of Mythology: The
    Myth of the Divine Child and the Mysteries of Eleusis* (R. F.
    C. Hull trans.) (London: Routledge and Kegan Paul).

3   Carl Gustav Jung and Karoly Kerényi, *Einführung in
    das Wesen der Mythologie*, 3rd edn (Zurich: Rhein-
    Verlag, 1951), p. 104.

4   Ibid., 137

5   Hetaera (or *hetaira*) in Attic Greek meant 'female com-
    panion' and was generally opposed to lawful wife,
    thus covering the entire range from courtesan to
    concubine.—Trans.

6   Jung and Kerényi, *Einführung in das Wesen der Mythologie*,
    p. 216.

7   Ibid., p. 255.

8   Ibid., p. 256.

9   Clement of Alexandria, *The Exhortation to the Greeks* (G.
    W. Butterworth ed. and trans.) (Cambridge and Lon-
    don: Loeb Classical Library, 1948), p. 34.

10 Most commonly referred to in English as the Graeae
(or Crones), they are the elderly and unageing sisters
and protectors of the Gorgons. They have a single eye
(and a single tooth) among them. Perseus forces them
to reveal their knowledge by stealing the single eye
while it is being passed from one sister to another.—
Trans.

11 Erwin Rohde, *Psyche*: *Seelencult und Unsterblichkeitsglaube
der Griechen*, VOL. 1 (Tübingen and Leipzig: Mohr
Siebeck, 1908), p. 289.

12 Clement of Alexandria, *Exhortation to the Greeks*, p. 30.

13 See Giorgio Colli, 'Eleusinia' in *La Sapienza greca, Volume 1*: *Dioniso, Apollo, Eleusi, Orfeo, Museo, Iperborei,
Enigma* (Milan: Adelphi, 1977), pp. 91–116.

14 Clement of Alexandria, *Exhortation to the Greeks*, p. 42.

15 The author is here alluding to the literal meaning of
infantile—of being 'without speech' (an idea explored
in a number of Agamben's earlier works, most
notably in *Infancy and History*, 1978).—Trans.

16 Rohde, *Psyche*, p. 289.

17 *The Works of Artistotle, Volume 12*: *Select Fragments* (translated into English under the editorship of David Ross)
(Oxford: Clarendon Press, 1952), p. 87.

18 The *kykeon* was a drink made from water, barley and
pennyroyal used by the Eleusinian mystery cult.—
Trans.

19 Hippolytus, *Contre les heresies* (P. Nautin ed.) (Paris: Les
Editions du Cerf, 1949), pp. 5, 8, 39–40.

20 Karoly Kerényi, *Die Mythologie der Griechen*: *Die Götter- und Menschheitsgeschichten* (Zurich: Rhein-Verlag, 1951), p. 238.

21 Clement of Alexandria, *Exhortation to the Greeks*, p. 36.

22 Odo Casel, 'Mysteriengegenwart', *Jahrbuch für Liturgiewissenschaft* 8 (1928): 146.

23 Lucius Apuleius, *The Golden Ass*: *Being the Metamorphoses of Lucius Apuleius* (W. Aldington trans., revised by S. Gaselee) (Cambridge, MA: Loeb Classical Library, 1915), p. 574.

24 Gianni Carchia, *Dall'apparenza al mistero* (Milan: Celuc libri, 1983).

25 Edgar Wind, *Pagan Mysteries of the Renaissance* (Harmondsworth: Penguin Books, 1967). pp. 15, 16.

26 Jung and Kerényi, *Einführung in das Wesen der Mythologie*, p. 153.

27 G. W. F. Hegel, *Werke in zwanzig Bände, Band 1*: *Frühe Schriften*, (Suhrkamp: Frankfurt am Main, 1986), pp. 231–3.

28 G. W. F. Hegel. *Phenomenology of Spirit* (A. V. Miller trans.) (Oxford: Clarendon Press, 1977), p. 65.

29 Colli, *La sapienza greca*, p. 382.

30 Ibid., p. 383.

31 Ibid.

32 Ibid., p. 15.

33 Rohde, *Psyche*, p. 299.

34 Ibid., pp. 290–1.

35 Jung and Kerényi, *Einführung in das Wesen der Mythologie*, p. 219.

Kore: Ancient Sources

Edited by Monica Ferrando

> *Tu me fai rimembrar dove e qual era*
> *Proserpina nel tempo che perdette*
> *La madre lei, ed ella primavera*

> You make me remember where and what
> Persephone was at the time when
> Her mother lost her, and she the spring

Dante, *Purgatorio* 28.49–51

All selections and translations for the original Italian edition (*La ragazza indicibile*: *Mito e mistero di Kore*, Electa, 2010) were done by Monica Ferrando. The English translations to follow attempt not only to be true to the original Greek and Latin sources but also to reflect Monica Ferrando's translations into the Italian.

Euripides, frag. 63 Kovacs

> The unspeakable girl

Euripides, *Helen* 1036–7

> The disappearance / of the unspeakable girl

Carcinus in *Didorus Siculus* 5.4–5

> Demeter's unspeakable girl

Plato, *Cratylus* 404c–e

> PHERREPHATTA: Many people are afraid to pro-
> nounce her name, and Apollo's. I suppose it is
> through ignorance of that which determines the
> fitness of names that they think of Persephone, the
> 'bringer of death', who is terrible to them. But, in
> fact, the name indicates that the goddess is wise.
> You see, since things are in motion (*pheromena*), that
> which grasps (*ephaptomenon*) and touches (*epaphon*)
> and is able to follow them is wisdom. Pherepapha,
> or something similiar, would thus be the correct
> name of the goddess, because she is wise and
> touches that which is in motion (*epaphe tou pherome-
> nou*). This is the reason Hades, who is wise, consorts

with her, because she, too, is wise. But people have altered her name, attaching more importance to euphony than to truth, and they call her Pherephatta.

Porphyry, *De abstinentia* 4.16

Most theology derives the name Ferrefatta (*Pherrephattes*) from 'nurturing the doves', because the dove is sacred to her. And so the priests of Maia consecrate a dove to her. Maia is identified with Persephone because *maia* means 'nurse'. And to Maia they also consecrate the cock . . .

HADES

Plato, *Cratylus* 403

SOCRATES. As for Pluto (*Ploutonos*), the name certainly derives from 'the giver of riches' (*tou ploutou dosin*), since his riches are buried in the bosom of the earth. As for the other name, Hades (*Haides*), most people think that means 'the invisible' (*to aeides*); and because they are frightened by the latter name, they say Pluto.

HERMOGENES. But what do you think about it, Socrates?

soc. As for me, I think that people mislead themselves about the power of this god and fear him wrongly for several reasons. They fear him because once we are dead we stay with him always; and they also live in fear of him because the soul goes to him stripped of the body. But it seems to me that this leads to one point—the office and the name of the king of the gods.

her. How?

soc. I will tell you what it seems like to me. Tell me, which is the strongest bond to hold a living being wherever he may be—is it desire or compulsion?

her. Desire, Socrates. By a great margin.

soc. And you believe that many would escape from that god if he had not bound those who go to him with the strongest of bonds?

her. Clearly.

soc. And so he must bind them, it seems, with some kind of desire, if he binds them with the most enduring of bonds and not compulsion.

her. It seems to me, yes.

SOC. There are many kinds of desire, aren't there?

HER. Surely.

SOC. Then he binds them with the strongest of all the desires, if he wants to bind them with the strongest bond.

HER. Yes.

SOC. And could there be a greater desire than to become a better man through association with some other person?

HER. By Zeus, there can be none greater, Socrates.

SOC. Then, Hermogenes, we must believe that this why no one has been willing to come away from that other world, not even the Sirens (*oude autas tas Seirenas*), but they and all others have been overcome by his enchantments, so beautiful, it appears, are the words which Hades has the power to speak; and from this point of view, this god is a perfect sophist and a great benefactor of those in his realm, he who also bestows such great blessings upon us who are on earth; such abundance surrounds him there below, and for this reason he is called Pluto. Then, too, he refuses to consort with them while they have bodies, but only accepts their souls when they are pure of all the vices and passions of the body. Does he not seem to you a philosopher, and to understand perfectly that, under these conditions, he could restrain them by binding them with the desire of virtue but that so long as they are infected with the unrest and madness of the body, not even his father, Kronos, could hold them to himself, though he bound them with his famous chains?

HER. Maybe you're not wrong, Socrates.

SOC. And the name Hades is not derived from 'the invisible', but more probably from 'knowing all noble things' (*alla polu mallon apo tou panta ta kala eidenai*)—for that reason he was called Hades by the lawgiver.

DEMETER

Homeri Hymnus in Cererem 1–2

I sing of Demeter of the beautiful hair, a sacred goddess (*Demeter eukomon semnen theon archorn' aeidein*) and of her delicate-ankled daughter (*auten ede thugatra tanisphyron*).

Plato, *Cratylus* 403

> soc. For the gift of food she brings with her,
> Demeter (*Demetra*) seems to have been referred to
> as 'she who gives like a mother' (*didousa os meter
> Demeter keklesthai*).

Papyrus Barolinensis 44, saec. II a. Chr. N. (F 49 Kern)[1]

> The goddess Demeter / . . . of Demeter / . . . her
> enemy / Orpheus has passed it down from Zeus
> as sister, / others, instead, as mother; of these, nei-
> ther / was destined for the memory of the loyal
> gods / . . . / It is I, Demeter, who make the sea-
> sons, by whom splendid / gifts are brought. What
> celestial god or mortal man / raped Persephone
> and betrayed her beloved heart? (*leghei gar: eimi de
> Demeter orephoros aglaodoros; tis theos uranios ee thneton
> anthropon / erpase Phersephonen kaiheon philon epahe
> thymon?*)

Apollodorus, *Library* 1.5.1

> Then she made her way to Celeus who ruled the
> Eleusinians . . . Celeus' wife, Metanira, had a child
> that was given to Demeter to raise; the goddess,
> wishing to make it immortal, set the infant on fire

at night to strip off its mortal flesh. But as Demophon—for that was the child's name—grew marvellously by day, [Metanira] came to watch, and when she saw him in the flames she cried out—the child was consumed by the fire and the goddess revealed herself.

But for Triptolemus, the eldest of Metanira's children, Demeter made a chariot pulled by winged dragons, and gave him wheat, with which he sowed the whole inhabited earth by wafting it through the sky. Panyasis affirms that Triptolemus was a son of Eleusis, for he says that Demeter came to him.

KORE OF THE COSMOS

Nonnos of Panopolis, *Dionysiaca* 4.101–102

As for the fate of the sons of the girl / the starry Virgin (*Parthenos astraie*) holds out a hand full of corn.

Stobeus, *Eclogae Physicae et Ethicae* 1.3–12

From the sacred book of Hermes Trismegistus, of her whom they call Kore of the Cosmos:

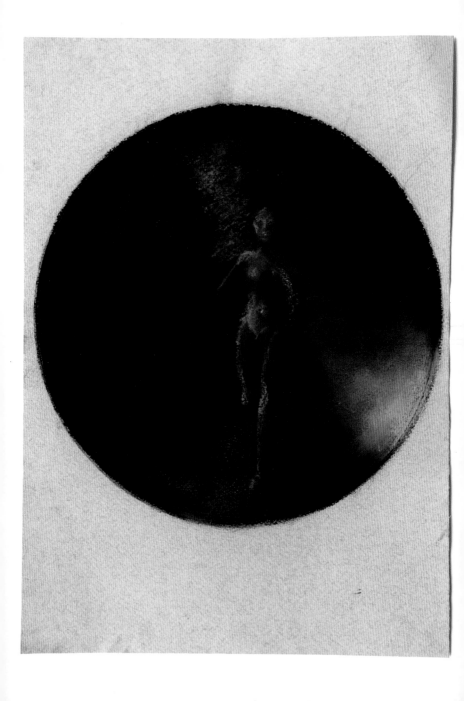

With the name 'Kore of the Cosmos', the figure of Kore appears to have been interwoven with that of Isis and with the image of the pupil of the eye, so that in Greek one says *kore*.[2]

QUEEN OF HELL

Demeter and Persephone were called 'Ladies' (*Potniai*), which refers back to a Cretan source of their cult which passed through Arcadia, where the veneration of Despoina—daughter of Poseidon and Demeter, who mated in the shape of horses—was diffused. From Crete, the cult of the 'Lady of the Animals' arrived in Arcadia, moderated in *Potnia Theron* as an attribute of Artemis but whose unnameability, in Arcadia, referred back to the unnameability of Kore-Persephone in Eleusis. The bond that links Crete, Arcadia and Eleusis, in this way, seems to be the accompaniment of the god by an animal in various forms: Torus–Pasiphaë in Crete, Poseidon–Demeter in Arcadia, Zeus–Kore in Eleusis.

Pindar, *Olympian Odes* 14.21

To the black-walled house of Persephone go now, Echo

63

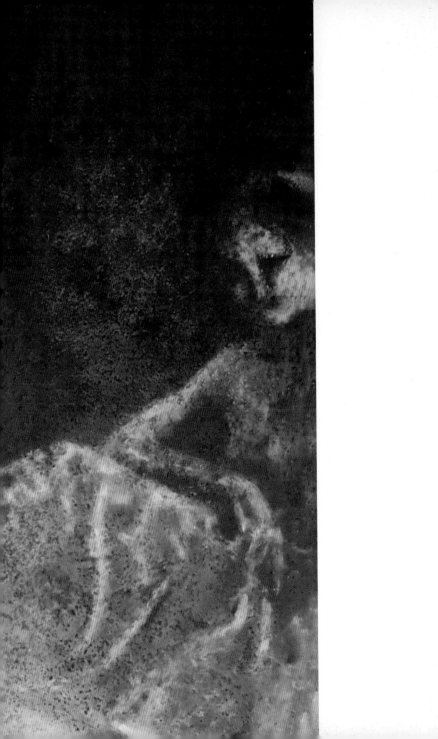

Pindar, frag. 133

> And, as for those from whom Persephone receives requital for her ancient grief: in the ninth year, she restores their souls to the splendour of the sun, and from them arise virtuous kings, and great men known for their strength and wisdom, and for the rest of time they are called sacred heroes among men.

Lamella Thuriis reperta 547k

> [A]nd Protogonos and Metis. To the mother of all things said / Kore, of the line of Cybele as much as of Demeter / [. . . O Zeus . . . O Sun, Fire, across / the city . . . you go . . . Victory / and Fortune also go, Phanes, Moira, whom / All remember . . . you, glorious demon . . . /. . . all things can be overthrown, all things / . . . in requiting, to subject / . . . not in the air of fire . . . mother . . . and for you . . . / Seven nights of fasting or after the day . . . / For seven days I fast for you, O Zeus / From Olympus, all-seeing, always . . . hear, mother / my prayer . . . and together, my beauty] / . . . Demeter, Fire, Zeus and the / Beneath . . . / at the mother's breast . . . / . . . at the mother's breast

Euripides, *Phoenician Women* 687

> I call you, call with a barbarian's voice, / O! with
> a barbarian's prayer: / Come, come to the land
> that / your descendants settled in here, and the
> two goddesses united in name: Persephone and
> the beloved goddess Demeter, who nurtures all
> and is queen of all, have won it for their own;
> escort the torch-bearing goddesses, defend this
> land; all things are easy for the gods.

Sophocles, *Oedipus at Colonnus* 1050

> This is the way shown by Hermes and the goddess
> of the underworld.

Lamella Thuriis reperta F 32d–e Kern, saec. IV–III a.
Chr. N. (National Archaeological Museum of Naples)

> Pure, I come from the pure, O Queen of Hell, /
> [Eucle and Eubuleus and all you other immortal
> gods, / since I flatter myself that I belong to your
> line, / your blessedness; / and I paid the penalty
> for the actions no more than just, / so that Moira
> or the dusk of thunderbolts crushed me]. And,
> now, I stay as a supplicant before Persephone the
> chaste, because she sent me benevolently to the

seat of the pure (*nun d'hiketis iko par'agnen Phersephoneian*). / Pure, I come from the pure, O Queen of Hell, / Eucle and Eubuleus and you other demons, / since I flatter myself that I belong to your line, / your blessedness; / and I atoned for unjust actions whether Moira will crush me, or the lightning. / And now I stay as a supplicant before Persephone (*nun de iketis eko para Phersephoneian*), / because kindly she sent me to the seat of the pure.

Plato, *Laws* 796b

And here, too, as for the woman-girl

E de au par'emin kore kai despoina

Diodorus Siculus 4.25.1–4 (Dindorf-Vogel)

And since we have spoken of Orpheus . . . He shared, too, in the Argonauts' expedition, and for the love of a wife he had the incredible courage to descend to Hades and, softening Persephone with his melody, he persuaded her to favour his desires and to allow him to bring back his woman from Hades, who was already dead, just as it happened to Dionysus.

Virgil, *Georgics* 4.486–487

And now, revived, she returned to the bright air /
Eurydice, raised by him and following him / as
Persephone had ruled it.

*Redditaque Eurydice superas veniebat ad auras / Pone
sequens—namque hanc dederate Proserpina legem—*

Virgil, *Aeneid* 4.136–143

Concealed in a tree without light, / in the leaves
and the flexuous branches, there is a branch of
gold / said to be sacred to Juno of Hell; she keeps
it all hidden, / the wood and the shadows huddle
in the obscure valleys. / But entry to the secret
recesses of the earth was forbidden / to those who
had not first torn down the golden offshoot of the
tree. / This was the gift the beautiful Persephone
claimed for hers.

*Latet arbore opaca / aureus et foliis et lento vimine ramus,
/ Iunoni infernae dictus sacer; hunc tegit omnis / lucus, et
obscuris claudunt convallibus umbrae. / Sed non ante datur
telluris operta subire, / Auricomos quam quis decerpserit
arbore fetus. / Hoc sibi Proserpina munus / Instituit*

Horace, *Satires* 2.5.109–110

> But Queen Persephone calls me
>
> *sed me / imperiosa trahit Proserpina*

Apollodorus, *Library* 1.3.1

> Hera, wife of Zeus, whence Hebe and Ares—but she combines with many other women both mortal and immortal. From Temi, daughter of Uranus, are born the Furies: Irene, Eunomia and Dike, and the Fates: Clotho, Lachesis, Atropos; from Dione is born Aphrodite; from Eurynome, daughter of the Ocean, the Graces: Aglaia, Euphrosyne and Talia; from Stygian Persephone (*ek de Stugos Persefone*); from Mnemosyne the Muses: Calliope, first, and then Clio, Melpo-mene, Euterpe, Erato, Terpsichore, Urania, Talia, Polyhymnia.

Claudian, *De raptu Proserpinae*

> From the depths, / Juno, sing with fierce song of the marriage bed
>
> *Profundae / Iunonis talamo audaci promere cantu*

The Celestial Weaver

Porphyry, *De antro nympharum* 14 (Nauck 66.13–19)

> And for the soul, the body is a garment it has donned . . . so, too, was Kore called by Orpheus . . . she has come to be remembered as a weaver, and the ancients say that the heavens, too, are a cloth, the garment of the celestial gods.

> *Kai chiton ghe to soma tei psychei ho emphiestai . . . houto kai para toi Ophei e Kore . . . istourgousa paradedotai, ton palaion kain ton ouranon peplon eirekoton oion theon ouranion periblema.*

Claudian, *De raptu Proserpinae* 246–270

> Persephone, soothing the house with sweet song / sewed in vain a gift against her mother's return. / Here her needle traced out the ordering of the elements / and the seat of the High Father, against whose laws Mother Nature / devised ancient chaos, and the first principles of things as they disposed themselves / in their proper places: light bodies were lifted high, / while heavy bodies drew down into the centre. The aether brightened, / the fire fled to heaven, the sea crashed open and the earth hung in space. / And her colours were not single.

In gold she picked out the stars, scattered purple
through the waters. / She seeded gems through
the waves, / and the clever threads that marked
the rolling waves / up-swelled.

Proclus, *In Platonis Timaeum* 41b–c (Diehl 3.223.3–9)

[A]nd therefore Orpheus says that the cause that
renders divisible things alive, which remains on
high and spins out the order of the heavens, is a
virgin nymph associated with Jupiter who stays in
her house, but who, one time, left her web incomplete, was torn by force from her home, taken by
force to be married, married to give birth.

kai dia tauta ara Opheus ten ton meriston zoopoion aitian
ano menousan kai yphainoustan ton diakosmon ton uranion
nymphen te heinai phesin os achranton kai tauta toi Dii
synaphtheisan kai menein en oikeiois ethesi, proelthousan de
apo ton heautes oikon atenei te kataleipein tous istous kai
armazeshtai kai anarpashtheisan gamaisthai kai gamethe-
isan ghennan

Proclus, *In Platonis Timaeum* 41b–c (Diehl 1.134.26–29)

[T]he cloth . . . which the goddess spun out
together with the father

o peplos . . . hon e theos yphainei meta tou patros

Proclus, *In Platonis Cratylum* 387e (Pasquali 22.2–3)

> Since Kore and all the chorus were dancing for
> she who remains on high, for she who spins the
> cosmic order of life
>
> *kai gar haute kai pas hautes ho choros ano menouses*
> *yphainein legontai ton diakosmon tes zoes*

Damascus, *De principiis* 339 (Ruelle 2.200.14)

> [D]escending perhaps from that which Orpheus
> called the meta-cosmic weaving of the cloth
> worked by Kore
>
> *apo tes par' Orphei Korikes yperkosmiou peplopoiias*
> *ormethentes*

Nonnos of Panopolis, *Dionysiaca* 6.128–154

> And where that river had bathed Cyane the
> maiden / and offered her his waters as a bride gift,
> in a whirlpool of springs / once he had finally seen
> her unveiled, / she saw a grotto like a high house
> / crowned and concealed with a great stone,
> which nature had sealed / with a door-like rock
> and set with a stone loom for the nymphs. / The
> goddess passed through the darkness of the cavern
> / and concealed her daughter well-secured in the

hollow rock. / Then she loosed the dragons from the winged car / and placed one to the right of the stone door / and the other on the left near the rocky threshold / to protect Persephone who was not easy to see. / There, also, she left Calligeneia, her devoted nurse / with her baskets and all that knowing Pallas gives to make women sweat at the loom. / With her feet she cut the air, / leaving her rounded chariot to the hermit nymphs of the rock. / With the sharp teeth of the iron comb the girl busied herself, / carding tufts of wool that clenched themselves tight round the distaff. / With impetuous twistings, in the hum of their spiralling / she guided the spinning dance of the threads as they drew together, to a centre. / And with restless feet back and forth / she ordered the first threads of the warp, where the work begins, / and turned them on the beam. / And then the girl set to plying the bobbin along through the threads and slope of the veil, / singing low to her cousin, Athena the Spinner, for whom the cloth was meant.

ANTHOLOGEIN OR THE GATHERING OF FLOWERS

Homeri Hymnus in Cererem 5–16

While playing with the girls of the flowering bosoms, the daughters of the Ocean, / and collecting (*anthea ainymenen*) / roses, crocus and beautiful violets (*hroda kai krokon ed'ia kala*), / in the sweet meadow (*leimon am'malachon*), / and iris and hyacinth (*kai agallidas ed'hyakinthon*); / and the narcissus, which was grown as a trap for the girl with the face like a rose (*narkisson th', hon physe dolon kalykopidikoure*), / by Gaia, in accordance with Zeus' desire to please the god of many guests; / miraculous flower, a glorious sight / that day, for all (*thaumaston ganoonta, sebas tote pasin idesthai*), / immortal gods as well as mortal humans. / From its root were lifted a hundred blossoms (*tou kai apo rithes hekaton kara exepephykei*) / and at its thick perfume the full breadth of the heavens smiled, and all the earth, and the salt orchards of the sea. Astonished, she reached out with both hands / to take the lovely bauble (*he d'ara thambesas' orexato hersin ham' ampho / kalon athyrma labein*).

Papyrus Barolinensis 44, saec. II a. Chr. N. (F 49 Kern)[3]

Of these things nothing / was intended for the memory of the devoted; take indeed / the origin of the daughter of Zeus and Demeter, Persephone, / who was braiding violets in the presence of / Ocean's daughters, who were called in Orpheus' poetry (*echei gare Dios kai Demetros thugatros archen / Phersephone iaplekouses sumparounson / ton Okean ous thugateron*): / Leucippe (*Leukippe*: shining) / Fanera (*Phanere*: brightening) and Electra (*Elektra*: blazing) and Ianthe (*Ianthe*: sea violet) / Melbosi (*Melobosis*: strophe) and Tyche (*Tyche*: fate) and Ociroe (*Okuroe*: swift current) with the blooming visage, / Chrysides (*Chryseis*: gold) and Ianera (*Ianeira*: the cleanser) and Acaste (*Akaste*) and Admete (*Admete*: untamed) / and Rhodope (rosy: *Rodope*) and Pluto (*Pluoto*: wealth) and the loveable Calypso (*Kalypso*: hidden) / and Stygian (*Styx*: frozen) Urania (*Urania*: heavenly) and Galassaura (*Galaxaure*: spring of water white as milk) / loveable / daughter of the narcissus, to which Kore, struck by its wonder, was / drawn, and with her two hands desired / to pluck . . .

In a loving band we arrange / the fat cups of the crocus and the hyacinth / (*tattomen erasthenti d'en tainiai kroku ed' yakinthu a kalykas euphengheias*) / for near them we must weave with our hands the seductive / flowers of the narcissus (*epei plekteon cheiress' eroenta pros authos narkissu anthen*)—that were made to bloom for the girl with the face of blooming flowers (*ha physe kalykopidi kuren*) / by Earth, by the will of Zeus, bestower of grace, according to Polydectes. / And then a venerable wonder for all who witnessed it, for immortals and mortal / men, and from the root of the narcissus were born a hundred crowns (*thaumaston ganoonta, sebas tote pasin idesthai athanatois te theois ede thnetois / anthropois, tu kai apo rizes hekaton kara exepephykei*).

Diodorus Siculus 5.3.1–4

And the violets of which we spoke and the rest of the flowers that infused the air with such perfume bloomed ceaselessly, each its own miracle, throughout the year, so that every aspect of the place was that of flowers and delight. And both Athena and Artemis, the myth continues, who had chosen like Kore to remain maidens, were with her and accompanied her as she gathered flowers, and all together they prepared the cloth for Zeus their father.

Ovid, *Metamorphoses* 5.391–394

> Spring is eternal. In the wood, Persephone was amusing herself collecting violets or white lilies, filling her little baskets and the folds of her garments with them, and vying with her companions to see who could gather more.

Plutarch, *Naturales Quaestiones* 23

> Therefore, no one in Sicily, they say, goes hunting near Etna, because all year a great quantity of mountain violets grow and bloom in the meadows, and the fragrance that fills the place overwhelms the odours exhaled by the animals. But, there is also that traditional story according to which Etna was the scene of the rape of Kore, while she was gathering flowers, and that is why people honour and revere that place as a sanctuary, and do not threaten the animals that live there.

Scholia in Sophoclis Oedipum Coloneum 681

> That does not mean that the narcissus was the crown of Demeter and Kore, for they were to have been crowned with spikes; . . . but it is possible that Sophocles might have said that the narcissus was an ancient crown of the great goddesses, using the

plural, instead of saying that it was an ancient crown of the goddess, that is, of Kore . . . because before she was raped by Pluto it pleased her—they say she was raped while gathering this flower—to such a degree that it was at one time one of her symbols, as if that flower was dear to her as a crown, before the rape. Which is to say, that later the goddesses made at least some crowns of flowers and also that it is prohibited for women celebrating the Thesmophoria to wear crowns of flowers. On his part, Istrus says that the garland of Demeter was composed of myrtle and yew.

Athanaeus, *Deipnosophistae* 12.533–534

Now, Clearcus of Solus in his *Amatoria (Erotikois)* says: 'Why do we gather in our hands flowers and fruits and things of that sort? Does nature seek to bring to the light those who desire beauty through our love for those things? Is this the reason—a sort of revelation offered by nature—that those certain persons who carry fruit and flowers in their hands joy in them? . . . It is, in fact, perfectly natural that those who think themselves beautiful and ripe for love gather flowers (*physikon gar de ti to tous ousmenous einai kalos kai ophairous anthologhein*).

Thus the girls in Persephone's train are also said to have been gathering flowers; and Sappho says: 'A very tender girl it is who gathers flowers.' (*othen hai te perì ten Phersephonen anthologhein legontai kai Sappho phesin idein anthe amergousan paid agan hapalan*)

RAPE AND DESCENT

Homeri Hymnus in Cererem 2–3

[T]he girl of the delicate ankles, whom Hades / raped (*en Aidoneus heraxen*)—Zeus, who sees far, planned it from his deep thundercloud, / eluding Demeter of the black spade (*Demetros chrusaorou*), goddess of the splendid harvests (*aglaokarpou*) / while playing with the girls of the flowery bosoms, the daughters of Ocean (*paizousan kouresi syn Okeanu bathykolpois*).

Homeri Hymnus in Cererem 15–39

Astonished, she reached out with both hands / to take the lovely bauble, but the earth opened, split with broad ways / the plain of Nysa (*chane de chthuon euryaguia / Nysion am'pedion*); there sprung the god who receives many guests (*te orousen anax polydegmon*), with his immortal horses, the son of

Kronos, who has many names. / And he placed
her away on his golden chariot, and through her
tears and sighs he bore her away; she cried pierc-
ingly / calling to her father, son of Kronos, highest
and best. / But not one of the immortals, or of
human mortals / heard her voice, not even the
olive nymphs, who bear such splendid fruit. /
Only the daughter of Perseus, the one who puri-
fied her mind / Hecate of the luminous diadem,
in her cave, / and the divine Helios, magnificent
son of Hyperion, / heard the daughter calling
upon her father, the son of Kronos: but these; /
and he was seated far from the gods, inside a tem-
ple of many prayers, / receiving gorgeous rites
from mortal humans. / And so, at the behest of
Zeus, the struggling goddess was taken / by him
who is lord of many, and who has many guests, /
her father's brother, / the son of Kronos, who has
many names, with the immortal horses. / So long
as the goddess saw the earth and the starry heavens, / the fish-heavy sea and its vast currents, /
and the rays of the sun, she waited for the return
of her beloved mother / and the company of the
gods who live in eternity, and although she was

worried hope soothed her noble heart . . . / The peaks of the mountains and the depths of the sea resounded / with her immortal voice, and her beloved mother heard.

Hesiod, *Theogony* 912–914

Then he mounted the marriage bed of Demeter the bounteous, / who bore Persephone of the white arms (*he teke Phersephonen leukolenon*); that Hades / ripped from her mother, wise Zeus having willed it

Marmor Parium (T 221 Kern); Jacoby 239 A 14 (*Die Fragmente der griechischen Historiker* II B 995.5–8)

Now, Orpheus, son of Egrus and Calliope displayed true poetry, of the rape of Kore and of Demeter's search and of the divine passion of those who had eaten the fruit (*ten eautou poesin exetheke, Kores te arpaghen kai Demetros*), in the year 1135, when the King of Athens was Erechtheus.

Papyrus Barolinensis 44, saec. II a. Chr. N. (F 49 Kern)[4]

[The] narcissus, to which Kore, struck by its wonder, was / drawn: and with her two hands desired / to pluck, in that moment it is said that the earth

/ opened and that up from the depths Hades came on his chariot and setting to his horses / took Kore away (*narkissu, eph'an e Kore thambesasa epedramen*; / *kai de taues tais chersin bulomenes / anaspasasthai auton, tote leghetai ten ghen / chanein kai ek ghes ton Aidonea anabanta / eph'harmatos kai eph' hippon sunarpasanta / ten Koren apagaghein*); and that Zeus with thunder and with lightning called up black horses / that arranged themselves like the shooting swarms of Artemis / . . . of Athena . . . of a sow, / that ended as had been planned by the judge / Dysaules; Kore, however, was weeping over what had happened / and . . . was derided by those who had been playing with her; after / she had heard the cries, Demeter / come from Sicily was wandering, / having come into the city she made herself invisible (*e de Kore epiachen eip tei tuchei, / me . . . n . . . nos . . . kai ton sunpaizuson kataghelastheie*; *epei / de de ekuses tes ghegonuias e Demeter, / ek Sikelias exelthusa esplanato, kata / basa de peri ten polin aphanes ghegonen*) on the plane of Nysa, where the lord who welcomes many guests made his spring with his immortal / horses, the son of Kronos, of many names. / Now, as long as the earth and the heaven / full of stars appeared above the goddess / still she hoped to see her beloved mother and the company of the ever-living gods. / And, too, Demeter, not so recently questioned by Hecate, said . . .

Ovid, *Metamorphoses* 5.395–401

Almost as soon as he saw her he took her: thus sudden was Pluto's love. The terrified goddess cried in mourning for her mother and for her company—but for her mother above all else—and since she had ripped the upper edge of her tunic, it loosened and the flowers she had gathered fell to the ground; and so great was the simplicity of her virgin heart that even the loss of those flowers was a wound.

Pausanias, *Description of Greece* 38.5

At Eleusis flows a Cephisus which is more violent than the Cephisus mentioned above, and near it is a place they[5] called Erineus, saying that Pluto descended there to the lower world after having raped the Maiden (*kai pa'auto kalousin Erineon, legontes ton Ploutona hote herpase ten Koren katabenai taute*). In the *Theaetetus* 143b, Plato situates the meeting of Theaetetus and Socrates in Erineus. It is possible that he intended to place the theme of the dialogue in relation with the rape of Kore.[6]

Diodorus Siculus 5.4.2–5

And the rape of Kore, the myth recounts, took place in the meadows that surround Etna. The site was near the city, a place of moving beauty for its violets and for every kind of flower, and worthy of the goddesses. And the story tells also that, because of the intensity of the flowers' fragrance, the hunting dogs could not follow the tracks of their prey; their odour was confused with it. And the meadow in question is level at its centre and well irrigated, but at the edges it rises and falls back to a cliff at each side. It is regarded as though it were the centre of an island, and for this reason certain writers call it the navel of Sicily. According to them, there are also sacred groves surrounded by shrubs, and a giant cavern through which runs a chasm that stretches through the heart of the earth and opens in the north; and it was through this, according to the myth, that Pluto emerged with his chariot to carry out the rape of Kore (*ten arpaghen tes Kores*).

Diodorus Siculus 5.3.4–4

> [B]ut a great stream was consecrated to Kore in the territory of Syracuse and it was given the name of Cyane or 'The Blue Fountain'. Indeed, the myth tells that it was near Syracuse that Pluto carried out the rape of Kore and took her away on his chariot and after he closed the earth again he descended into Hades bearing with him the wife he had abducted and from the fountain called Cyane came water.

Diodorus Siculus 5.5–5

> That the rape of Kore took place in the way that we have described is attested to by many ancient historians and poets. In Carcinus the tragic poet, for example, who often went to Syracuse and was a witness to the zeal with which its inhabitants organized the sacrifices and festivals in honour of Demeter and Kore, we find the following verses:

> 'They say of Demeter's unspeakable girl (*Demetros pot'arreton koren*) / that Pluto, so they believe, raped her in secret / and then vanished into the black light of the abysses of the earth.'

Apollodorus, *Library* 1.5.1

> Pluto fell in love with Persephone and with Zeus'
> help he raped her in secret.

> *Plouton de Persefones erastheis Dios sunergountos erase*
> *auten krufa*

DEMETER'S SEARCH

Homeri Hymnus in Cererem 40–74

> An acute sorrow seized her soul; from her divine
> / hair she tore with her hands her diadem, / she
> threw over her shoulders a mourning veil, / and
> she threw herself over the hard earth and the sea
> like a wild bird / to the search. But none of the
> gods, no mortal humans wanted to tell her the
> truth, / and none of the birds came to her with
> true messages. / For nine days, then, the venerable
> Demeter wandered / over the earth, turning in
> her hands burning torches; / and nothing of
> ambrosia or nectar, sweet drinks, / did she take, /
> lost in her sorrow, nor did she step into the bath.
> / But when at last, on the tenth day, the fulgent
> dawn arrived / Hecate came to her, bearing a
> torch in hand; / and, wanting to inform her, she

spoke to her and said: / 'Venerable Demeter, bringer of the harvest, of magnificent gifts, / who among the celestial gods or among mortal men / has raped Persephone, and has seeded the worry in your heart? / Indeed, I heard the scream, but I did not see the rapist / with my own eyes. / I have told you all, in brevity and truth.' / Thus spoke Hecate, and she did not answer, / the daughter of Rhea of the beautiful hair; instead, she moved with her, set out with her, turning flaming torches in her hands. / And they sought out Helios, who watches over gods and men; / they stood in front of his horses / and the most divine of the goddesses asked him: 'Helios, you at least have respect for a goddess like me, if ever / my words or my deeds were pleasing to your heart and your soul. / The daughter whom I bore, my sweet seedling, with the luminous face . . . I have heard her high cry pierce the limpid aether, / as if she had been forced, but I did not see it with my eyes. / But since you, certainly, with your rays, / see all the earth and the sea from the divine aether, / tell me truly if you have not seen / who took my precious daughter by force, against her will, while I was far

away, / and then fled, whether it be one of
the gods or one of the mortal men.' / Thus she
spoke . . .

Homeri Hymnus in Cererem 74–90

And thus responded the son of Hyperion: /
'August Demeter, daughter of Rhea of the beautiful hair, / you will know the answer: I do respect
you profoundly and sympathize with you, / anx-
ious like you for the delicate-ankled girl. No one
else / among the immortals is responsible, if not
Zeus the cloud-bearer, / who destined her to be
the flowering wife of his own brother, Hades, and
down into the sooty shadows / he has taken her
with his horses, after he raped her and she
screamed as loud as she could. / But you, O goddess, cease your flood of grief: it is not fit / that
you should feed a rancour without end. He is not
below you, as a son-in-law, among the immortals,
Hades the god of many guests, / your brother,
who shares your blood; and as for honour / that
he obtained when, at the beginning, / the three-
part division was made; / and he abides with those
whom he touches, and over them he is king.' /
After having thus spoken, he spurred his horses;

and at his call they drew the swift chariot like
long-winged birds; / but through the heart of the
goddess went a sorrow, an ache.

Euripides, *Helen* 1301–1352

Once, then, the mountain mother of the gods
went running swift-footed along the wooded
groves and the fleet course of the rivers and the
deep-thundering waves of the sea, yearning for
her lost daughter, the unspeakable girl.

*Oreia pote dromadi kolo mater theon esube / an ulante nape
/ potamion te cheum'udaton / barubromon te kum' alion
/ potho tas apoichomenas / arretou kouros*

And the clamour of rattlesnakes resounded and
came to a crescendo; and beside the deathless
goddess and her chariot drawn by wild creatures,
two goddesses appeared, to help her find the
girl snatched from the dances of her friends—to
run with her, swifter than storms, Artemis with her
bow and Gorgon-faced Athena with her spear.
But Zeus, who sees far from his throne in heaven,
brought a different destiny to pass. And when in the
exhaustion of her wandering course the mother
had put a stop to the search for her daughter, taken

by trickery and borne away without a trace, she pushed herself through the clouds that cover the mountain home of the nymphs of Ida, and for sorrow she pressed herself into the snowy woods. Now, with the fields no longer fertile for the good of mortals, without vegetation and without fruit, she let human beings die and no longer made the opulent plantations bloom. She clipped the delicate herbs. Life in the city ceased, and the sacrifices to the gods—on the altars no more offerings burnt. And the fountains of pure water were stopped by the goddess, oblivious in their streamings of her daughter's rape.

But, just as for humankind, so for the gods, all festivals and sacrifices were abolished, and Zeus, who wanted to give solace to the bleak mother, spoke thus: 'Go, holy Charities, chase away the sadness of the Goddess in agony over the loss of her daughter, chase it away with your shouts of joy, and you, Muses, with the songs of your choruses.' And Kypris, the most beautiful goddess, sounded for the first time the deep voice of bronze and took up the tambourines of well-stretched hide; and the mother began to smile and took in her hands the low-pitched flute.

Carcinus in *Diodorus Siculus* 5.4.5–5

[L]onging for the vanished girl, / her mother searched for her and journeyed through every region / and in the country of Sicily, and in the lands of Etna, / full of fire that scorched the way / in the most fiery places / humankind in sorrow for the girl / denied the harvest, but faithful to Zeus consumed them. / From then unto today they honour the goddesses.

Callimachus, frag. 466 Pfeiffer

Callimachus literally says this: 'United with Demeter, Zeus bred Hecate, who is known among the gods for her strength and stature. He says that she was sent with them by her father underground to seek Persephone (*en ypo ghen pempthenai ypo tu patros pros Persephones zetesin phesin*), therefore, now, also she is called Artemis and Protector and Bearer of Torches and Bearer of Light and Chythonia.

Ovid, *Fasti* 4.577–579

Parrhasian stars (that can know all / since you are never submerged under the waters of the sea), show this wretched mother her Persephone!

Parrhasides stellae (namque omnia nosse potestis, / aequoreas numquam cum subeatis aquas), / Persephonen natam miserae monstrate parenti!

Diodorus Siculus 5.4.2–5

After the rape of Kore, the myth proceeds, Demeter, incapable of finding her daughter, took torches from the crater of Etna and went through the many regions inhabited by humans, and to those who welcomed her with goodwill she distributed blessings, rewarding them with the gift of harvest.

Apollodorus, *Library* 1.5.1

Demeter went searching over the earth entire, from day to night, by the light of torches, but when she came to know from the inhabitants of Hermion that Pluto had raped her, she was angry with the gods and abandoned heaven and, assuming the aspect of a mortal woman, she took herself to Eleusis. First, she seated herself on a rock that, from its appearance, was called Agelasto (*Aghelaston*) according to the madman called Callicorus (*Kallichoron*).

ELEUSIS: THE GIRL AT THE FOUNTAIN

Homeri Hymnus in Cererem 91–178

And later, enraged with the son of Kronos, of the
black clouds, / she abandoned the company of
the gods and vast Olympus, / and went through
human cities and their fertile fields, / hiding her
face for a long time; and no one recognized her,
not one of the men / or the slender women she
met, / until she came to the house of the sage
Celeus, / who then reigned over incense-clouded
Eleusis. / She was sitting by the road, stricken in
her heart, / at the well of the Virgin, where the
inhabitants of the city drew water, / in the shade,
under the thick branch of an olive tree. / She was
like that ancient woman, far past motherhood, /
and far from the gifts of Aphrodite, who loves gar-
lands in a woman's hair; / she was like those
nursemaids of the sons of kings who attend to justice, / and in the halls of echoing palaces dispense
the same. / And she was seen by the daughters of
Celeus, son of Eleusis, / come to draw the water
that was flowing abundantly to carry it / in bronze
water-jars to the house of their father. / They

were four, like goddesses, in the flower of youth: /
Callidice, Cleisidice, the loveable Demonassa and
Callithoe, who was the oldest among them, / and
they did not know her—difficult it is for mortals
to know gods . . . Thus she spoke, and the goddess
accepted with a nod; and the girls, / having filled
their shining jars with water, took them home,
exulting. / Swiftly they came to the house of their
father, and without pausing they told their mother
/ what they had seen and heard; and she at once
/ sent them, to go and bring the woman, promis-
ing a great reward. / As deer or heifers in spring,
/ who leap full-bellied through the meadows, / so
they gathered up the hems of their garments, /
running along the rutted street, and their hair /
fell over their shoulders like the blossoms of
crocuses.

Papyrus Barolinensis 44, saec. II a. Chr. N. (F 49 Kern)[7]

[W]ounded, she was sighing for her daughter. But
Calliope and Cleisidice / and Demonassa together
with the queen were walking to draw water and
asked themselves if it could be Demeter / as a mortal, while they approached: so says Museus in his
poetry. In his discourses he has to search for a

reason / to receive the blessing of the gods (*En tois logois dei ten aitian aitein met'euerghesian theon*).

ELEUSIS: IAMBE OR BAUBO

Homeri Hymnus in Cererem 197–205

There she was sitting, with her hands holding her veil over her face; / and for a long time, silent and full of distress, she remained immobile in her chair, / and returned to no one a word or a gesture, / but without smiling and without tasting food or drink, aching for the return of her slender girl; / finally the hardworking Iambe with her banter, joking continuously, induced the venerable goddess / to smile, to laugh and to clear her heart, / Iambe, who was dear to the goddess' spirit ever after

Philiscus of Corcyra 680.54–62

[B]ut the crone, Alinunte, who was above mountain customs, at the right moment / sent for a case ... for those worthy of honour was the naughty conversation perhaps without advantage? / Indeed upright, she cried, loudly and with courage; she did not throw her herbs for goats / not for this was the goddess hungry . . . but the ambrosia sustained her delicate belly

Papyrus Barolinensis 44, saec. II a. Chr. N. (F 49 Kern)[8]

And Baubo gave her the child to raise / and invited her to the house. Demeter then, having already promised to lodge in the house with the child, raised it / as its nurse, and after having greased the child with ambrosia / she laid it all night in the fire / and just at / morning / she took it back, to hide the thing from its parents. And the child / did not want to nurse or to take other food, / but it was well fed and lovely; stunned / by the growth of the child, one night, Baubo / she saw, through the door, that the goddess / was carelessly leaving the child in the flames, and realized then / that secret rites were unfolding.

Apollodorus, *Library* 1.5.1

[T]hen she brought from Celeus who then reigned in Eleusis; there were women who invited her to sit near them, and there was a crone named Iambe, who, making obscene gestures, provoked the goddess' laughter. And this is why the women make obscene gestures during Tesmophoria.

Clement of Alexandria, *Protrepticon* 2.20–21 (Staehlin 1.15.23–16.7)

Indeed Demeter, wandering in the search for her daughter Kore, turns to Eleusis—a place belonging to Attica—tires herself and sits sadly near a well. To go there is now prohibited to the initiates, lest they seem to imitate the goddess in her sorrow; and at that time Eleusis was inhabited by its natives: their names were Baubo and Dysaules and Triptolemus, and also Eumolpos and Eubuleus. Triptolemus was a herdsman, Eumolpos was a shepherd and Eubuleus a swineherd; from these descended the line of the Eumolpidae and of the Kerykes (the Heralds), who form the group of hierophants at Athens. And, in truth, Baubo—for I will not hesitate to say it—welcomes Demeter as a guest, and offers her the *kykeon*. But she refuses to take it, she will not drink for heartache. Baubo is hurt and, thinking she has been slighted, exposes her genitals to the goddess. And Demeter cheers up, and finally accepts the drink—she is pleased at the sight. Such are the occult mysteries of the Athenians. These things, you see, Orpheus also records. And I will

cite the same verses to you, so that this mystagogue can prove his shamelessness:

This said she drew aside her robes and showed all the clefts / of her body, ashamed by nothing: and there was Iacchus, / and laughing he pressed his hand under Baubo's breasts / and at this the goddess smiled, she brightened in her heart, / and accepted the shining cup of kykeon.

John Tzetzes, *In Aristophanis Plutum* 1013, column B

The Athenian women, while they were returning on their chariots to celebrate the mysteries, were trading abuses, and this was called 'the abuse of the chariot'. They were abusing each other as to how much it was that, when Demeter arrived at Eleusis for the first time in search of Kore, prey to anxiety, Iambe, the servant of Celeus and Metanira, by covering her with abuses, pushed her to smile, and made her also accept food, which was the *kykeon*, of fine flour mixed with water and boiled.

Eleusis: The Rite

Homeri Hymnus in Cererem 207–211

> [H]e said, that in truth it was forbidden / to drink the red wine, and commanded that as a drink / water be offered with barley flour mixed with delicate mint. / The woman prepared the *kykeon* (*he de kykeo teuxasa*), and she gave it to the goddess as it had been ordered. / Demeter, the most venerated, accepted it, and commenced the rite (*dexamene d'osies*).

Homeri Hymnus in Cererem 268–274

> I am the august Demeter, she who is greater than all others, / to all immortals and mortals I offer joy and comfort. / Well then, a great temple, and in it an altar, / all the populace shall build at the foot of the Acropolis and its sublime wall, / higher than the well of Callicorus, on the top of the hill; / I myself will teach you the rite, so that in the future / you can celebrate piously to placate my spirit.

Homeri Hymnus in Cererem 472–482

> All the spread of the earth was covered / with foliage and flowers; she stood in the way, and taught the kings that render justice /—to Triptolemus and

Diocles, driver of horses, / to the strong Eumolpos, to Celeus lord of the people—/ the means of the sacred rite; and revealed the solemn mysteries—/ and in worshipping in no way was it allowed to profane, to ask questions, / or to answer, as when confronted with the gods great wonder silences the voice. / Happy among humans who live on earth, those who were admitted to the rite! / But those who were not initiated into the mysteries, those who were excluded, will never share such a sweet fate, not after death, when they go down into shadows and squalor.

Herodotus 8.65.4

Diceus . . . responded: 'Every year the Athenians celebrate a festival in honour of the Mother and her Daughter and those who would like to be among them and the other Greeks have come to be initiated; the voice that you hear is the invocation to the stone (*lakko*) they raise every year for this festival.'

Aristophanes, *Thesmoforiazusae* 1148–1152

Come propitiously, benevolently, Ladies, into your sacred wood, / to those who are not permitted to see / the venerable rites of the two goddesses because they shine / like the light of lamps, immortal visions.

Philiscus of Corcyra 676

For Chythonian Demeter, for Persephone and for Climene the gifts are mysteries.

Philiscus of Corcyra 680.36–53

At Eleusis, the cry of the rock that leads the many worshippers / and the procession that welcomes those who have completed a long journey to the waves of the sea / nourished by you they grease the olive branches / one stream of water for each of the two goddesses / with your tears you will make a fountain flow / flowing regally / we will do deeds / that outdo words / we vow to sway the unbelieving / now they carry the branch of supplication / pouring it again / in the festival of the initiation / to succeed in the highest / guided by you Persephone to see the stars / if I guide you, you will never fall / lift high the pine torches, relax the furrowed brow. / He ceases speaking and they rise, the Nymphs and the Graces, devoted to the just persuasion; all the horde of women express proper reverence, pressing their foreheads to the earth / to cover the goddess with leaves they take up the few plants remaining in the sterile earth.

Papyrus Barolinensis 44, saec. II a. Chr. N. (F 49 Kern)[9]

And Celeus, having left the fields, / for the city . . . / . . . throwing . . . / The mother, that is, the stranger / The daughter . . . / The sea for the mother . . . / But Demeter . . . saying / Of the transgression . . . / That has authority over all . . . / Left . . . of the voice . . . / Saw the black horses . . . / . . . god . . . of / Mystery . . . sow . . . the *kykeon* / Was drunk, until the . . . / To Triptolemus . . . / So that it is called 'The Descent'

Pausanias 1.38.1

The so-called Rheitoi are like rivers only by their course, for their water is salt . . . which means to say that the Rheitoi are sacred to Kore and Demeter, and above all to the priests to whom it is granted to net fish there. In ancient times, as I know, they constituted the border between Eleusis and the rest of the Attic territories.

Hippolytus, *Refutatio omnium haeresium* 5.8.41–43 (Marcovich) (F 352 Kern)

> Then there is the mystery of Eleusis and 'Anacto-rium': Eleusis because we who are full of the breath come from on high and travel through the most high. This . . . is that which the initiates at Eleusis call the great mysteries. Normally, . . . he who is initiated into the lesser mysteries comes in time to be initiated in the great mysteries also: 'Fate from the greatest death has arisen even greater.' Lesser . . . are the mysteries of Perse-phone, the mysteries of the underworld.

Proclus, *In Platonis Cratylum* 402d (Pasquali 85.22–23)

> [. . .] and so they say also that Kore was violated by Zeus and raped by Pluto
>
> *dio kai prasi ten Koren ypo men tou Dios Bazesthai, hypo de tou Ploutonos arpazesthai*

Porphyry, frag. 360f

> In the mysteries of Eleusis the hierophant dresses in the image of a demiurge, the highest priest in the image of the sun and the priest of the altar in the image of the moon. The sacred herald is dressed as Hermes.

Proclus, *In Platonis Rem Publicam* 1.125.21–22

> [. . .] sacred lamentations, pronounced in secret,
> of Kore and Demeter and even of the greatest
> goddess have passed down the initiations

THE EARTH WITHOUT FLOWERS
AND WITHOUT FRUIT

Homeri Hymnus in Cererem 302–313

> [A]nd the blonde Demeter, / seated in the temple,
> remained apart from all the gods, / aching with
> regret for her slender, lost daughter. / And on the
> fecund earth she made that ill-omened year /
> terrible for humankind: no more did the soil / let
> the seeds germinate; thus did she keep them
> hidden underground, Demeter of the beautiful
> headdress. / Many a curved plow was dragged in
> vain by many an ox across the fields, / many a
> white grain fell to nothing in the earth. / And cer-
> tainly she would have entirely destroyed the
> human race / with inexorable hunger, and the
> splendid privilege of offerings / and of sacrifices
> would have been taken from those who live on
> Olympus, if Zeus had not taken care, and had not
> meditated in his heart.

Homeri Hymnus in Cererem 331–333

> She said she would never return to fragrant Olympus / and would not consent to the growing of fruit on the earth, / before she had seen with her own eyes the girl with the beautiful face.

WEDDING IN HELL

Homeri Hymnus in Cererem 334–345

> From his deep thundercloud Zeus, who sees far, / sent to Erebus the slayer of Argos, with the golden wand, to convince Hades with apt words / to lead the venerable Persephone out of the dense shadows / to the light of day, among the gods, so that her mother could see with her eyes and put aside her anger. / Hermes obeyed, and swiftly from the earth to the depths / he hurtled, leaving the house of Olympus. / He found the god there in his house, sitting on his throne with his noble companion / who was full of worry and disquiet at the memory of her mother—and her mother, pressed to it by the intolerable will of the immortals, was thinking of her terrible plan.

Callimachus, frag. 43.117 Pfeiffer (Etymologicum Gudanium B [= Etymologicum Symeonis Codex 5 = Etymologicum Magnum p. 406.46])

> Zagreus is Dionysus, according to the poets; indeed it seems that Zeus united with Persephone (*dokei gar ho Zeus mighenai tei Persephonei*), from which was born the chthonic Dionysus (*ex es chthonios o Dionysos*). Callimachus says: the daughter who birthed Dionysus Zagreus (*hui Dionyson Zagrea gheinamene*)

Ovid, *Fasti* 4.587–604

> 'If you remember by whom Persephone was born, she / ought to have half of your heart. / . . . the rapist enjoys the fruit of his crime. / But neither did Persephone deserve a predator for a husband / nor should we prepare for her a son this way . . .' / Jove tried to soothe her, and excused the deed by naming love. / And he said: 'He is not a son-in-law we cannot be proud of; / . . . But if in this case your spirit will not be consoled / and your only wish is to break those bonds of wedlock, / let us try to break them . . . but only if she has kept her fast. / If not she will be the wife of her infernal spouse for ever.'

Ovid, *Metamorphoses* 5.504–508

> Passing below the earth through the gorges of
> Styx, I saw down there, with my own eyes, our
> Persephone: sorrowful, yes, and also a little terri-
> fied, / but in all aspects queen of the dark world,
> powerful consort of the sovereign of Hell.

> *Ergo dum Stygio sub terris gurgite labor, / visa tua est*
> *oculis illic Proserpina nostris: / illa quidem tristis, neque*
> *adhuc interrita vultu, / sed regina tamen, sed opaci maxima*
> *mundi, / sed tamen inferni pollens matrona tyranni*

Athenagoras, *Pro Christianis* 20.3–4 (Schoedel)

> [. . .] how Zeus persecuted his mother Rhea when
> she refused to wed him and how, after she became
> a serpent, he too became a serpent . . . and wound
> himself into her. The rod of Hermes symbolizes
> this union. And then Zeus mated with his daugh-
> ter, Persephone, in the shape of a serpent taking,
> too, she who birthed his son Dionysus. (*eith' oti*
> *Phersephonei tei thug atri emighe bissamenos kai tauten en*
> *drakuntos schemasti, ex es pais Dionysos autoi*)

Proclus, *Theologia Platonica* II, 6, III, 371

> Since the theological accounts that pass down the
> most sacred rites of the worshippers at Eleusis say

that Kore remains above in the home of her mother, and that below she reigns in Hell with Pluto . . . Kore is mingled with Zeus and Pluto, first . . . in so much as he took her by violence, and second in that he raped the goddess. (*he Kore Dii men kai Ploutoni synesti, toi men . . . biasamenoi, toi de arpasanti ten theon*)

Proclus, *In Platonis Cratylum* 406b (Pasquali 106.5–9)

Thus Kore, in keeping with Artemis and Athena, whom she followed, is said to be a virgin girl. But in keeping with the power and fertility of Persephone herself it is said that she might receive and couple with the third demiurge, and birth, as Orpheus says, nine shiny eyed daughters, flower-urgers.

Hothen de kai he Kore kata men ten Artemin ten en eautei kai ten Athenan parthenos leghetai menein, kata de ten tes Persephones gonimon dyamin kai prosienai thugateras glaukopidas anthesiourgous

Proclus, *In Platonis Cratylum* 404e (Pasquali 96.12–23)

Great indeed was the similarity between these two lines, that of Kore and that of Apollo . . . Since, according to Orpheus, Demeter says, trusting her reign to Kore (*polle gar estin he koinonia ton duo touton-seiron, tes Korike lego kai tes Apolloniakes . . . dio kai par' Orphei he Demeter encheirizousa tei Korei ten basilieian phesin*): But mounting the flowery marriage bed of Apollo, / you will make shining sons, with faces of burning fire.

Proclus, *In Platonis Cratylum* 404d (Pasquali 95.10–15)

Since she is also called Persephone, precisely to the degree that she unites with Pluto (*dio kai Perse-phone kaleitai malista toi Ploutoni synousa*) . . . and was wedded to Hades and together they generated the Eumenides who live in the underworld

Apollodorus, *Library* 1.5.1

But Persephone was made to stay with Pluto for a third of each year; the rest of the year she passed among the gods.

Persefonen de kath'hekaston eniauton to men triton metà Ploutonos henkasthe menein, to do loipon para tois theoi

Nonnos of Panopolis, *Dionysiaca* 6.155–165

[. . .] virgin Persephone, nor could you escape your nuptials, (*parthene Persephoneia, su d'ougamoneures alyxai*) / and a dragon was your mate / when

Zeus, taking that serpentine form, wanted you, /
writing in spirals, full of desire / came in with
the darkness into your girl's room, / mouthing
thickly, after having put to sleep / the eyes of the
dragons like him / who were guarding the door. /
And with wooing lips he licked your girl's body /
full of sweetness (*Kai gamiais genuessi demas lichmazeto
koures meilichos*). / Filled by the heavenly serpent /
the belly of Persephone swelled with a rich birth,
/ yielding Zagreus, born with horns.

Pollux 1.37

The Theogamy and the Anthesteria of Kore held
by the Siculi

Kores para Sikeliotais Theogamia kai Anthesporia

Claudian, *De raptu Proserpinae* 2.277–306

'Cease, Persephone, to torture your heart with
heavy grief / and in vain fear. You will have a
greater kingdom, nor will your spouse be unwor-
thy of you. / I am the offspring of Saturn, to
me the order of things obeys / and my power
stretches through the immensity of the void. / Do
not believe you have lost the light: we have other
stars, other orbits; you will see a purer light /
and

wonder at Elysium's sun and blessed inhabitants: there humankind is most noble, / there lives a golden race and we possess forever / that which the earthly win only once. / You shall have soft meadows, and only the sweetest breezes, and ever-blooming flowers such as Enna never produced. / And in a thick forest there is a precious tree / whose curving branches gleam with living ore; / the tree is consecrated to you, you will be found queen of blessed autumn and rich with golden fruit. / But I have as yet said little: whatever the limpid air embraces, whatever the rich earth nourishes, the salt seas sweep, / the rivers roll, or the marshlands feed, / all living things alike will be your subjects, / all, I say, that dwell beneath the moon, the seventh of the planets, that in its ethereal journey separates mortal life from the deathless stars. / To your feet will come kings in purple / stripped of their splendour, and mixing with the poor / (death renders all equal!). / You will condemn the guilty, / you will give rest to the virtuous. To your justice the wicked will confess the crimes of their lives. / Accept the Fates for your handmaidens, with the waters of Lethe / and what you will shall pass.

Desine funestis animum, Proserpina, curis / et vano vexare metu. Maiora dabuntur / sceptra nec indigni taedas patiere mariti, / Ille ego Saturni proles, cui machina rerum / servit et inmensum tendit per inane potesta. / Amissum ne crede diem: sunt altera nobis / sidera, sunt orbe salii, lumenque videbis / purious. Elysiumque magis mirabere solem / cultoresque pios: illic pretiosior aetas, / aurea progenies habitat, seperque tenemus / quod superi meruere semel. Nec mollia desunt / prata tibi: Zephyris illic melioribus halant / perpetui flores, quos nec tua protulit Henna, / Est etiam lucis arbor praedives opacis / fulgentes viridi ramos vurvata metallo: / haec tibi sacra datur fortunatumque tenebis / autumnum et fulvis semper ditabere pomis, / Parva loquor: quidquid liguidus complectitur aer, / quidquid alit tellus, quidquid maris aequora verrunt / quod fluvii volvunt, quod nurtivere paludes, cuncta tuis pariter cedent animalia regnis / lunari subjecta globo, qui septimus auras / ambite et aeternis mortalia separat astris, / Sub tua purpurei venient vestigia reges / deposito luxu turba cum paupere mixti / (omnia mors aequat!): tu damnatura nocentes, / tu requiem latura piis; te iudice sontes / improba cogentur vitae commissa fateri, / Accipe Lethaeo famulas cum gurgite Parcas, / sit fatum quodcumque voles

Claudian, *De raptu Proserpinae* 2.362–372

[. . .] the virgin is led to the marriage bed. She is watched / over by Night in her starry mantle, who, touching the bed, consecrates it to unending union and the hope / of sons. / The souls in the kingdom of Dis exult / and with their sleepless acclaim they begin the song: / 'Powerful Juno of the mortals and you, brother and son-in-law / of Thunder, take now the union of sleeping as one / and in your embracing weave together both your hopes. / Now bear blessed offspring; happy Nature is waiting / for the next gods. Bring new divinity into / the world and give to Ceres the grandchildren she desires.'

Ducitur in thalamum virgo. Stat pronumba iuxta / Stellantes Nox picta sinus tangesque cubile / omina perpetuo genitalia foedere sancit, / exultant cum voce pii Ditisque sub aula / talia pervigili sumunt exordia plausu: 'Nostra potens Iuno turque o germane Tonantis / et gener, unanimi consortia dsicite somni / mutuaque alternis innectite vota lacertis. / Iam felix oritur proles: iam laeta futuros / Expectat Natura deos. Nova numina rebus / Addite et optatos Cereri proferte nepotes

The Seed of the Pomegranate

Homeri Hymnus in Cererem 346–369

> And, moving close to him and stopping, the potent
> slayer of Argos spoke: / 'O Hades of the dark
> hair, who reigns over the dead, / Zeus, the father,
> ordered me to conduct from Erebus, / up among
> the gods the august Persephone, so that her
> mother can see her with her own eyes and put an
> end to her rancour and her inexorable rage /
> against the immortals; since she is planning a ter-
> rible project: / to the poor line of humans born
> on earth / holding the seed beneath the ground,
> and destroying the offerings / that the immortals
> expect.

Homeri Hymnus in Cererem 411–413

> [B]ut Hades, insidiously, / gave me the seed of the
> pomegranate (*embale moi roies kokkon, meliede edoden*),
> food sweet as honey, / and he forced me to eat it
> against my will

Ovid, *Fasti* 4.607–614

> 'The raped girl,' he said, 'broke her fast with three
> seeds / the pomegranate had stored in its supple

skin' / . . . if Jove had not promised / that Persephone would be in heaven for twice three months

*'Rapta tribus,' dixit 'solvet ieiunia granis, / Punica quae
lento cortice poma tegunt.' / . . . pactus nisi Iuppiter esset,
/ bis tribus ut caelo mensibus illa foret*

Apollodorus, *Library* 1.5.1

Zeus ordered Pluto to send Kore back to earth
and Pluto, so that she would not spend too much
time with her mother, gave her a seed of the
pomegranate to eat. She ate it, not knowing what
would come of it.

*Dio de Plouton ten Koren anapempsai keleusantos, o Plou-
ton, ina me polun chronon para te metri katameine, roias
edoken aute faghein kokkon. He de ou proidomene to sum-
beromeno katenalosen auton*

Scholia in Luciani Dialogos meretricios 2.1 (Rabe, p. 275)

The Thesmophoria is a Greek festival that includes
the mysteries and is also called the Scirophoria.
It was celebrated on the basis of a myth that
relates that when Kore was raped by Pluto while
gathering flowers, there was a swineherd named
Eubuleus in the same place, who was guiding his

swine over the meadow, and who was swallowed up with him in the chasm of Demeter and Kore. To honour Eubuleus, therefore, they throw piglets in the cave of Demeter and Kore.

Nonnos of Panopolis, *Dionysiaca* 4.90–101

Demeter, you who love your daughter, when from the cone of shadow the ray of light will be snatched from Selene, / guard Persephone from a rapacious spouse, / the hidden thief of the inviolable girl, / if the linen thread of the Parcae is obedient. / Unhoped for, you will see before night a furtive spouse, / a wild creature, sharp of mind, in the light of the setting sun, / with the lady of Paphos claimed by Hades the night-thief / and you will see the dragon they reared together. / The most blessed we call you; you of the four corners of the cosmos / will be famous for your splendid fruits, for you make fertile / the barren earth.

Pseudo-Clementine, *Homiliae* 6.9.5

They interpret, also . . . Demeter as the earth and Kore as the seed (*Koren eis spermata*)

Claudian, *De raptu Proserpinae* 2.204–5

> The nymphs fled. Prosperina was raped on the chariot / and cried to the goddesses for help.
>
> *Diffugiunt Nymphae: rapitur Proserpina curru / Imploratque deas*

THE RETURN OF KORE
AND THE FRUITS AND FLOWERS OF THE EARTH

Homeri Hymnus in Cererem 375–389

> And the immortal horses were harnessed to the chariot / by the lord of many men, Hades. / She mounted the chariot, and beside her sat the powerful slayer of Argos, / and taking into his hands the reins and the whip / he drove away from the palace; / willingly the horses took flight. / Swiftly they travelled the long way: neither the sea / nor the waters of the rivers / nor the grassy valleys, / slowed the speeding of the immortal horses, nor did the mountains; / much higher they went, slicing the dense clouds. / And after having driven there where Demeter of the beautiful headdress / was staying before a temple fragrant with incense. Seeing her daughter / the goddess threw herself

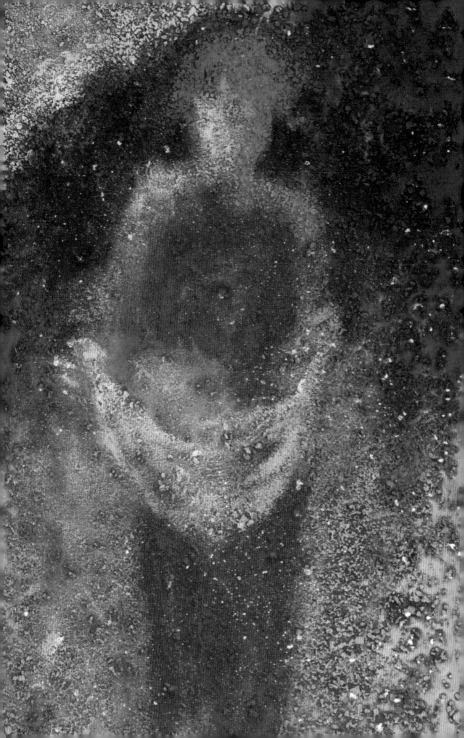

like a maenad down the woody mountainside. /
On her part Persephone, when she saw the beautiful face / of her mother, left the chariot and the
horses, / and coming down to her threw her arms
round her neck, clinging tight.

Homeri Hymnus in Cererem 401–403

Every time the earth covers itself with fragrant
flowers, / all the colours of spring, then from the
dense shadows / you spring anew, marvellous
bounty to the gods and to mortal humans.

Homeri Hymnus in Cererem 453–456

But in later times it was swiftly covered with long
shocks of grain-like hair, / as the spring advanced
/ and in the fields the fertile ruts began to over-
flow, and that which had been cut was bound up
in sheaves.

Homeri Hymnus in Cererem 470–473

[. . .] and Demeter of the beautiful headdress
obeyed, / and at once made the harvests of the
fields rich with sod. / All the wide earth was filled
with foliage and flowers.

Virgil, *Georgics* 1.38–39

> And no matter how the Greeks / admire the Elysian Fields and / if Persephone disdains her mother's call

Ovid, *Metamorphoses* 5.566–571

> [N]ow the goddess, the common divinity of two realms, passes half the year with her husband and her mother all the rest. Suddenly she changes, in spirit and aspect; for she who could seem sorrowful even to Dis now shines with joy, just as the sun, once covered by dark clouds, breaks through them, victorious.

> *nunc dea, regnorum numen commune duorum, / cum matre est totidem, totidem cum coniuge menses. / Vertitur extemplo facies et mentis et oris; / name, modo quae poeterat Diti quoque maestro videri, / laeta deae frons est, ut sol, qui tectis aquosis / nubibus ante fuit, victis e nubibus exit*

INITIATION INTO BLESSED LIFE

Lamella Thuriis reperta (F 32f Kern) saec. IV–II a. Chr. N. (National Archaeological Museum of Naples)

> But the soul had just abandoned the light of the sun, / on the right . . . hiding, she who knows / all

at once. / Rejoice, you have known passion: this / is not the first you have known. / From a man is born a god; lamb, you have fallen into milk. / Rejoice, rejoice in taking the road on the right / through the divine meadows and groves of Persephone. (*Chaire, chaire, devi odoiporon / leimonas te ierous kai alsea Phersephoneias*)

Proclus, *In Platonis Timaeum* 42c–d (Diehl 3.297.6–10)

[T]he holy life, far above the wanderings of birth, that which with Orpheus too the initiates of Dionysus and Kore boast of / *ten eudaimona . . . Zoen apo tes peri ten genesi planes, hes kai oi par' Orphei toi Dionysoi kai tei Korei teloumenoi tchein euchontai*): / to leave the cycle of birth and to keep faith in the mysteries

Proclus, *In Platonis Rem Publicam* 2.185.10–12 (Kroll)

And the most holy Eleusinian rites promise to the mystics the pleasure of the gifts of Kore, once they are liberated from their bodies.

Olympiodorous, *In Platonis Phaedonem* 67c (Norvin 43.15–20)

And also Kore is sent downward to Hades but is led by Demeter again upward, and her dwelling is that of before

kai he Kore de kataghetai men eis Hadou, anaghetai de
palin kai okei entha palai hen, hypo tes Demetros

Scholia in Sophoclis Oedipum Coloneum 1053 (Papa-
georgios 446.10–18)

And some say also that Eumolpos introduced the
rites celebrated each year at Eleusis for Demeter
and for Kore (*ten myesin ten syntelousmenen kat' enlauton*
en Eleusini Demetri kai Korei). Andronus writes that
it was not Eumolpos who introduced the rites but
another Eumolpos descended from the first, of the
fifth generation. From Eumolpos was born Cerice,
from Cerice Eumolpos, from Eumolpos Antiphemus, from Antiphemus the poet Museus and from
him came the Eumolpos who began the rites and
became a priest.

Orphei Hymnus XXXIX in Persephonem

Persephone, daughter of great Zeus, come, blessed
/ only begotten, gracious Goddess, receive these
rites / Pluto's venerable spouse, you are wise and
life-giving, / you hold the doors of Hades in the
depths of the earth. / Come to us ever, you of
lovely hair, sacred flower of God, / Mother of the
Eumenides, Queen of the Underworld, / whom
Zeus with unspeakable nuptials made to birth a

girl (*he Zeus arretoisi gonais teknosato kouren*), mother
of loud-shouting, many-shaped Eubuleus, play-
mate of the seasons, bringer of light, radiant
in form, / holy, ruler of the world, maiden who
showers down copious fruits (*semne, pantokrateira,
kore karpoisi bruousa*), resplendent, horned, sole
beloved of mortals. / You are spring, rejoicing in
fragrant meadows (*eiarine, leimoniasin chairousa
pnoesin*), / revealing your sacred presence in the
sprouting of green fields, / and in the autumn
time you are raped, taken back into your wedding
bed, / you alone are life and death to mortals and
their many woes, you who feed and slay all. /
Hear, blessed goddess, lift up your fruits from the
earth, / you who flourish in peace and in sweet
health, / and bring a happy life, that prospers into
age, through all your realms, Sovereign, and the
benevolence of Pluto.

Translated by Annie Julia Wyman

Notes

1   See 'Paraphrase eines Gedichtes über den Raub
    der Persephone' in *Berliner Klassikertexte* (F. Bücheler,
    W. Schubart and H. Diels eds). VOL. 5.1 (Berlin,
    1905).

2   Cf R. Reitszenstein, *Poinmandres: Studien zurgriechisch-
    aegyptischen und früchristlichen Literatur* (Leipzig: B. G.
    Teubner, 1996), pp. 145ff.

3   See 'Paraphrase eines Gedichtes über den Raub
    der Persephone' in *Berliner Klassikertexte.*

4   Ibid.

5   The Eleusinians and the Athenians.—Trans.

6   Cf. Ludwig Preller, *Griechische Mythologie* (Berlin,
    1894), p. 759.

7   See 'Paraphrase eines Gedichtes über den Raub
    der Persephone' in *Berliner Klassikertexte.*

8   Ibid.

9   Ibid.

THE PICTORIAL POETICS OF KORE

Monica Ferrando

Remove figure from ground, from the immemorial ground in which figures live their diaphanous lives like thin dreams. Shed light. Persuade the figures to leave the obscurity in which they lay mired and placid. Draw them out with colour and body. Find the right signs. Learn their infinite variety. Then forget it, as it is only the brush which, in *chi*, at the opportune moment, gives life to colour. Difficult.

Everything, even the figure on the pupil, is figured; everything is mobile, creative obscurity. It is there that the growing images nestle, hide, multiply.

Do not search for meaning as a means of fleeing the ordinary in the everyday. In the picture's absolute immediacy, the gift of light, fear dissipates and pretext disappears.

Kore: a single figure of many movements and faces. Unspeakable pupil. Kore is what you call the picture that emerges from Hades' darkness, driven by its generative force. The colours are Kore's seeds—her nature's substance.

Kore is in our culture's most treasured images and in the most ordinary things of everyday life. She is in the beautiful ways in which we clothe, unconsciously, the hours, in the ecstasy with which a certain season, mythically returning, reveals herself—in springtime.

Translated by Leland de la Durantaye